'*Cyclogeography*'s magic lies in the quality of the prose and Day's skill in looping together disparate threads in a way that feels natural . . . His many literary and philosophical detours make for an interesting ride.' – John Sunyer, *Financial Times*

'Jon Day's ode to the bicycle takes the reader pillion from petrol-choked city to rolling dale in eloquent prose, which at best pedals in beat to the accompanying landscape.' – Nicholas Hogg, *Independent*

'There's a gap in travel writing, and Jon Day has just zipped into it – like a bike courier between white van and black cab.' – Michael Kerr, *Telegraph*

Jon Day is a writer, academic and cyclist. He worked as a bicycle courier in London for several years, and now teaches English Literature at King's College London. His essays and reviews have appeared in the *London Review of Books*, the *Times Literary Supplement*, *n+1* and the *Guardian*. He writes about art for *Apollo*, and is a regular book critic for the *Financial Times* and the *Telegraph*. He is a contributing editor of *The Junket*, and a 2016 Man Booker Prize judge.

91120000306401

Jon Day

–

CYCLOGEOGRAPHY

Journeys of a London
Bicycle Courier

 Notting Hill Editions

Published in 2015
by Notting Hill Editions Ltd
Widworthy Barton Honiton Devon EX14 9JS
This paperback edition published in 2016

Designed by FLOK Design, Berlin, Germany
Typeset by CB editions, London

Printed in Poland on behalf of Latitude Press

Image credit on page 24: 'Room with a View' copyright © Benjamin
Hughes.
Image credit on page 115: Stressed Photograph, c.1950, Nigel Henderson
(1917–1985). Purchased 2007. © Nigel Henderson Estate. Photo credit:
© Tate, London 2015

A CIP record for this book
is available from the British Library

ISBN 978-1-910749-27-2

www.nottinghilleditions.com

for Dora

Contents

– Prologue –

The bicycle is half way between the shoe and the car, and its hybrid nature sets its rider on the margins of all possible surveillance. Its lightness allows the rider to sail past pedestrian eyes and be overlooked by motorized travellers. The cyclist, thus, possesses an extraordinary freedom: invisibility.

– Valeria Luiselli, 'Manifesto á Velo'

A few years ago, after finishing a degree, I was looking for a new job. I'd tried many: private tutor, mercenary essay-writer for the rich and lazy, barman, gardener, marketing consultant. Three months as a runner at a TV production company were enough of a taste of office life. Days spent tea caddying, photocopying and washing up left me cold. I couldn't drive, and my bosses told me I needed to learn if I wanted to get ahead in television. I arrived early and left late. Men carrying clipboards with radios strapped to their waists often shouted at me. I couldn't work the telephone system. I spent my afternoons shredding endless scripts on a temperamental shredder.

The only part of the job I did enjoy was the daily run to the edit suites in Soho, over the river from where

I worked, carrying the day's rushes – heavy blue tapes sheathed in their grey plastic wallets; volatile nitrate film adorned with 'no smoking' signs and warning skulls and crossbones; hard drives stuffed with data – which I did by bicycle. Soon I'd volunteer for any job taking me outside the office and across London, the further the better. Going to the archival warehouse to dig out old tapes or embarking on treks across the city for some specific prop became absurdly exhilarating. It was the solitude I valued, the freedom of the outside, the sounds and smells of the street. Soon I gave up my TV job and became a bicycle courier.

I'd grown up in London and had always loved to cycle. My Dutch mother and car-phobic father ensured I learned to ride a bike almost as soon as I could walk. They'd push me along the road by the scruff of my neck, riding beside me and steering me through gaps and around potholes with the delicate touch of puppeteers. The earliest bike I remember cycling under my own steam was a war-era, single speed machine with an iron frame and crumbling rubber grips. It was a faithful conspirator in my early explorations of the local territory. Together we built up our own map of the area – noting the location of a chipped kerbstone that allowed us effortlessly to ramp up onto the pavement; the green car, always parked in the same spot, which shielded our turn from oncoming traffic – charting features that felt as permanent as the roads we travelled over and the buildings we passed on our rounds.

When I became a bicycle courier I found that I loved cycling for my living. I loved the exhilaration of pedalling quickly through the city, flowing between stationary cars or weaving through the lines of moving traffic. I loved the mindlessness of the job, the absolute focus on the body in movement, the absence of office politics and cubicle-induced anxiety. I loved the blissful, annihilating exhaustion at the end of a day's work, the dead sleep haunted only by memories of the bicycle. By night I dreamt of half-remembered topographies, each point-to-point run connecting in an ever-expanding series. Sensations of falling were transformed into forward motion. Hypnogogic jerks, those juddery twitches that occur on the edges of deep sleep, were smoothed out into circular pedal-strokes of the legs.

Most of all I loved learning what London taxi drivers call 'the Knowledge': the intimate litany of street-names and business addresses that constitutes a private map of the city, parallel to that contained within the *A–Z* but written on the brain, read by leg and eye. After a while the trade routes became entrenched. By bike a new and unfamiliar London unveiled itself, a London dominated by road surfaces and traffic, a London composed of loading bays and stand-by spots, characterised by a sense of movement and flow. As a cyclist you inhabit the gaps between traffic, and as a courier you profit from what Jonathan Raban calls, in *Soft City*, 'the slack in the metropolitan economy'. The job allows you access to a subterranean world of cavernous loading bays and car parks burrowed away underground. It's the iceberg theory of architecture. Another city exists alongside the London most people know, and cycle couriers are privy to this backstage city, with its post rooms manned by neon-tabarded security guards, its goods lifts, its secret, parallel infrastructures.

Big commercial buildings can feel like miniature city-states, and to a cycle courier the conflict between public and private, between the rules of the road and those of corporate estates, is constantly apparent. The glee with which the police hunt down and fine couriers who jump red lights (while letting off their commuting counterparts) is well known. But the guardians of private land are just as intolerant. In the biggest developments access for couriers is restricted to the cargo bays. Hulking ramps and doors must be navigated, pictures are taken, ID cards printed off stating your name, company, purpose, and privileges.

Sometimes, proclamations of ownership are local and specific, as in the small 'Polite Notices', which read as anything but, informing you that 'Bicycles locked to these railings will be removed'. Elsewhere the limits of ownership spill out beyond the railings. Representatives of the 'West End Company' patrol Oxford Street in red hats, giving tourists directions and admonishing cyclists who ride on the pavements. Some large commercial estates, such as Devonshire Square off Bishopsgate in EC2, have their own private police force. Anyone who isn't obviously an office worker, snatching a lunchtime sandwich in the open air, is moved on. Running is forbidden.

I worked as a bicycle courier for three years, on and off, as I bided my time in between stretches back at university and tried to work out what to do with my life. I loved every moment of it. Or perhaps love is the wrong word. For after a while on the bike, doing this work, you simply *need* to carry on to feel normal. You feel ill if you don't work five days on the bike, anxious and twitchy when you take your feet off the pedals. You can't sleep without the weariness provided by the miles.

A bicycle courier's experience of London is formed by the demands and rhythms of capitalist circuits. Couriers occupy a contained space, the boundaries of which are fluid, established by the economic footprint of what our controllers – intermediaries between client and courier who take booked jobs and issue them over the radio to riders – contemptuously refer to as the 'push-bike circuit'. The rough borders of the circuit run round practical limits described by the confluence of physical capacity and the post-code system. Wapping, populated by exiles from Fleet Street, forms the eastern hub; Knightsbridge marks the Western front. There's usually not enough short-hop work to justify sending bicycles much further. The circuit doesn't penetrate far south. Occasionally I'd dash over the river, but, other than the odd outlying raid on Peckham or Stockwell, would never go much further south than Elephant and Castle. Mostly I'd skim along Southwark Street, working the edge of the river which was once the greatest trade route in London but is now lined only with the husks of trade: warehouses and docks re-purposed as office blocks and yuppie housing. To the North, the foothills of Camden, Highgate and Hampstead are the outer limits. There isn't much work above the economic tree line.

Cycling through the city everyday makes you learn not only its abstract properties – street names, business addresses, the locations in which policemen like to lurk and wait to catch you running red lights – but what it feels like to ride down a particular road in the wet (mapping the placement of slippery drain covers that wait to catch you out on sharp turns) or the dry; the specific sequence of lights at a much-crossed junction. As a courier you learn to inhabit the places in between the pickups and the drops. You learn the secret smells of the city: summer's burnt metallic tang; the sweetness of petrol; the earthy comfort of freshly laid tarmac. Some parts of London have their own smells, like olfactory postcodes. The Shisha bars on Edgeware road haze the area with sweet smoke; the mineral tang of Billingsgate fish market wafts over the Isle of Dogs.

Riding a bike for a living means you learn to read the road too, calculating routes, anticipating snarl-ups, dancing round potholes almost unconsciously. It is an activity that forces you to think of the city in literary terms. With its signs and painted hieroglyphics the road is an encyclopaedia of movement: drive here, walk here, park here, no stopping here. Look down and the tarmac tells you what to do. Traffic lights regulate the entire mechanism like enormous clocks, telling you when to move and when to stop. Textures too are important: kerbstones separate walkers from the flow of traffic; knobbled paving alerts the blind to a coming crossing. Very soon the rhythms of the street become internalised. Traffic lights and vehicle indicators, the wails of sirens and car alarms, warn you to get out of the way or lure you on. Eventually you come to feel part of the city's secret networks, at one with its hidden rivers and its dead-letter drops, at one remove from its anonymous crowds of commuters.

Alongside riding London I began to read it. I always kept a book in my bag for the slow days, and usually I sought out books that offered commentaries on my own working environment: anecdotal accounts of the city, or novels set in London, or histories of the city. Cycling itself felt like a form of interpretation – a mode of engaging with the urban text – and I also wanted to understand the strange and distinct attraction to place that I'd discovered by riding my bicycle, so I read about cycling too: biographies of the heroes of road racing, histories of the grand cycling Tours.

London is generally thought of as a walker's city. It's been written about from the perspective of the rambler and the stroller, but never much from the saddle. This lack represents a greater gap in travel writing, which is so often associated with shoe rather than saddle leather. Though there are 'a lot of walker-poets', as Paul Fournel – member of the avant-garde literary group Oulipo, keen cyclist and author of *Need for the Bike*, the best work of cyclophilosophy I know – has argued, the bicycle is less well represented as a literary vehicle. 'Cyclist-poets are less numerous' than walking poets, writes Fournel:

but that's due to inattentiveness, since the bike is a good place to work for a writer. First, he can sit down; then he's surrounded by windy silence, which airs out the brain and is favorable to meditation; finally, he produces with his legs a fair number of different rhythms, which are so much music to verse and prose.

I wondered if this oversight had something to do with the history of the bike. In *Wanderlust*, her wonderful history of pedestrianism, Rebecca Solnit argues that the act of walking for its own sake – and the tradition of writing about walking for its own sake – coincided with the rise of European Romanticism. Jean-Jacques Rousseau's idealised walk, in which leisured individuals could embark on journeys of their own volition, accompanied by bodies that were allies rather than traitors or burdens, and over terrain they were allowed free access to, was, Solnit says, the first example of a kind of ideological or philosophical pedestrianism which coincided with the rise of the city. For Rousseau walking was a tool that could be used to measure yourself against the natural world, a world that was coming into keener focus as urban life began to dominate human experience. You found your place within it by beating its bounds.

For the Romantics walking was an act of authorship too, a way of writing yourself onto the landscape and thus claiming it anew. Walking was democratic. Wordsworth privileged the act of walking not only because, as he said, his mind 'only worked' with his legs, but because as an act it created the paths and rights-of-way that would eventually be etched onto maps or fossilised in tarmac.

With the formation of the modern city the Romantic walker was transformed into the urban *flâneur,* the solitary (and generally male) 'stroller' who haunted nineteenth-century Paris, getting lost amongst its boulevards and arcades and documenting his experiences as he went. Yet unlike the Romantic walker the *flâneur* was a decadent figure, a leisured dandy who, freed from the demands of the rat-race, was able to spend his days at one remove from the mob, losing himself in the crowds of the city as he travelled amongst them. For him the city became reconfigured as a spectacle: buildings could be as sublime as

mountains; streets were abstracted into riverine tor-
rents. The rural walker became urbanised. In 'The
Painter of Modern Life', an urtext of *flânerie*, Charles
Baudelaire described 'Monsieur G.', a figure based on
the artist Constantin Guys, the archetypal and original
flâneur. As Baudelaire wrote:

He marvels at the eternal beauty and the amazing harmony
of life in the capital cities, a harmony so providentially main-
tained amid the turmoil of human freedom. He gazes upon
the landscapes of the great cities – landscapes of stone, ca-
ressed by the mist or buffeted by the sun.

The *flâneur* treated both the city and its inhabitants
as inanimate objects to be viewed disinterestedly, as
though through glass (Walter Benjamin would base his
Arcades Project, a sacred text for contemporary *flâneurs*,
on the idea that modern urban life was best exemplified
by the figure of the window shopper). But the figure of
the *flâneur* also celebrated the subversiveness of walking, politicising pedestrianism (especially in cities which
were increasingly hostile to walkers) and celebrating
the slow, the meandering, and the directionless over
the concerted migrations of capitalism. The undirected
walk challenged the timetable. The stroll was opposed
to the commute. Flânerie represented a way of con-
fronting the endless flow of people who thronged the
city's streets twice a day, regular as clockwork, on their
ways to and from work. On foot, the *flâneur* avoided

the official channels of movement – the circulatory networks of tram and bus and train – choosing instead to inhabit the hinterlands and marginal areas of the city. For Benjamin the leisured status of the *flâneur* was a kind of political statement also. In *The Arcades Project* he argued that 'the idleness of the *flâneur* is a demonstration against the division of labour' and that 'basic to flânerie is the idea that the fruits of idleness are more precious than the fruits of labour.'

By the 1950s, these radical pedestrian impulses had been channelled into the loosely defined notion of 'psychogeography', a term coined by the sociologist Guy Debord and derived from his investigations with the *Situationist Internationale*, an avant-garde revolutionary group which organised various subversive happenings in mid-century Paris. Psychogeography was both a political call to arms and an urban thesis. It described both a mode of existing within the city and a methodology for researching it. At the heart of psychogeography was the practice of what Debord called the *dérive*, the 'drift', which he defined in his essay 'Theory of the Dérive' as 'a technique of passage through varied ambiances'. 'In a dérive,' Debord wrote:

one or more persons during a certain period drop their relations, their work and leisure activities, and all their other usual motives for movement and action, and let themselves be drawn by the attractions of the terrain and the encounters they find there.

For Debord, the *dérive* was a journey conducted on a whim, but it wasn't quite aimless. Although they may have been undirected, these walks were constrained in other ways: governed by arbitrary rubrics imposed in order to generate unlooked for surprises. The Situationists used maps of Paris to navigate Berlin, they followed psychologically resonant ambiences in the urban fabric, they drew crude symbols onto their maps of the city and went out to walk and document the routes those symbols described. Walking was the favoured mode of transport. From these journeys it was hoped might emerge, writes the archmagus of London psychogeography, the writer Iain Sinclair, 'dynamic shapes, with ambitions to achieve a life of their own, quite independent of their supposed author. Railway to pub to hospital: trace the line on the map. These botched runes, burnt into the script in the heat of creation, offer an alternative reading – a subterranean, preconscious text capable of divination and prophecy.'

Removed from the 'usual motives for movement' the psychogeographer was free to get lost in the stimulating *Gesamtkunstwerk* of the modern city, losing him or herself in the process, becoming one with tarmac and glass and steel. These journeys were neither work *nor* leisure, therefore, but psychic *research*. Debord imagined a time when people could be liberated from their intelligences and sensibilities so as to be released as aimless particles in urban space, to be blown where they may by the winds of association, set free to hunt for the hidden 'fissures in the urban network' as they went. In doing so they could, he thought, transcend the linearity of both the map and of the commute, un-covering a realm of unconsciously registered connec-tions and ambiences as they went.

Walking was good enough for Debord, but the bike, which came to maturity alongside the modern city, and which would seem to have been an obvious vehicle for him to make use of, was nowhere to be seen in the writings of the psychogeographers. In her 'Manifesto á Velo', the Mexican writer Valeria Luiselli recognises this lapse, arguing that the bicycle should be reclaimed from the single-issue fanatics – from the cycle couriers, commuters, rickshaw drivers and, above all, lycra-clad racing cyclists, who so often give it a bad name – and used as a tool for a purer form of urban exploration. 'Riding a bicycle is one of the few street activities that can still be thought of as an end in itself,' she writes:

The person who distinguishes himself from that purposeful crowd by conceiving it as such should be called a *cycleur*. And that person – who has discovered cycling to be an occupation with no interest in ultimate outcomes – knows he possesses a strange freedom which can only be compared with that of thinking or writing.

The longer I worked as a bicycle courier, the more I realised that the freedom of the *cycleur* – a pedalling equivalent of the *flâneur* – was implicit in the story of the bicycle itself. The history of cycling is the history of the modern landscape. Since their invention in the mid-Victorian era, bicycles have been associated with freedom, allowing previously immobile groups of people to become self-propelled and socially mobile, to discover the landscapes they inhabit. It has been said that the bicycle did more for the gene pool than the railways, allowing – perhaps for the first time in human history – the poor to leave their villages and mix with their near-neighbours. The bike was the first technology of mass mobilisation. It is a nostalgic technology but it is also forward-looking, utopian and hybrid, tempered both by the backward glances of a pastoral cycling tradition and by the mad futurist visions of F. T. Marinetti, Samuel Beckett and Flann O'Brien. The bike is a technology of Man fused with machine, but also of machine communing with landscape.

As Luiselli and Fournel argue, the lack of representation of the bicycle in travel writing is surprising, then, especially as there does seem to be something inherently literary about the act of cycling. Both cycling and writing are self-directed activities. If you stop working, you stop moving. The verb 'to spin' used to refer to the making of thread from fibre: spinning yarn on a wheel. Later it was applied to the motion of the wheel itself, and eventually the metaphor came full circle, describing the way in which stories themselves are told: spinning a yarn, stitching together a series of observations into one continuous, unbroken narrative. Cycling, like writing, forces you to think not just in terms of individual steps but in terms of conjunctions, routes and structures: how am I to get from here to there? How exactly will I navigate this particular snarl of metal and rubber and steel and chromium? How will I get to the end?

The rhythms of movement provided by cycling seem perfectly suited to the writer's need to notice. At bicycle-speed your eyes focus on a single scene as you glide past, and for a few seconds you can isolate one incident before you're rolled onward. Then on to the next. The saccades of the eye's-snatch-and-focus synchronise with your velocity, flicking from rubbish bin to lamppost, from bus swerving out in front of you to pedestrian about to cross the road behind. The bicycle provides a road's-eye view midway between the ponderous bus-gaze and the start/stop stress of the car. Driving, in the city at any rate, is binary, reverential, distancing. Cycling flows, converting static and isolated glimpses of the city into a moving, zoetropic flicker of life.

Finally, cycling is instinctive, making you *feel* a landscape rather than merely seeing it. By bike your environment writes itself onto your body. 'Certain configurations of field, road, weather and smell,' writes the historian Graham Robb, 'imprint themselves on the cycling brain with inexplicable clarity and return sometimes years later to pose their nebulous questions. A bicycle unrolls a 360-degree panorama of the land, allows the rider to register its gradual changes in gear ratios and muscle tension, and makes it hard to miss a single inch of it, from the tyre-lacerating suburbs of Paris to the Mistral-blasted plains of Provence.'

Urban cyclists live in Euclidian cities, hidden to others, cities made up of inclines and angles, curves and cambers. Almost unconsciously cycling uncovers the deeper and older structures of a landscape than car or train travel can. 'The itinerary of a cyclist,' Robb continues, 'recreates, as if by chance, much older journeys: transhumance trails, Gallo-Roman trade routes, pilgrim paths, river confluences that have disappeared in industrial wasteland, valleys and ridge roads that used to be busy with pedlars and migrants.' Sometimes getting on a bike can feel like a kind of time-travel. The needs of the cyclist – gentle inclines, quiet roads, protection from the wind – have more in common with those of cattle drivers or pilgrims than they do with most contemporary travellers. We seek the same routes.

Despite the inherent constraints of the courier's journeys, therefore, after a while I realised that the job could provide just as liberating a way of encountering urban space as walking could. After a few months on the road as a courier I began to think of each run as a *dérive*, and each day's work as an act of cyclogeography.

My life as a courier became a hymn to measurement. Distance travelled equalled money earned. Calorific intake (measured in 'burger units', the international scale of energy: 5,000 calories for a hard day's pedalling, half that for a slow one) and effort expended tallied with monetary remuneration.

True, my journeys weren't completely arbitrary, conducted according to the artifices and rituals of psychogeographic attraction. As a courier your journeys are never really your own. They are the products of trade rather than leisure. Nor were they particularly symbolic or mystical. I didn't inscribe abstract shapes onto the map and pedal them out, or attempt to follow any significant or resonant routes. And yet they were equally dependent on happenstance. Unlike the *flâneur*'s unfocused yet reverential strolls, my journeys were conducted at the whims of capitalism and guided by the decisions of my controllers, articulated on the tarmac by the instinctive gestures of body and bicycle. Though my journeys were imposed from above they were still unauthored. Or rather, perhaps, it was better to think of the city authoring these journeys itself: writing them through a confluence of economic demand and the curious idiosyncrasies of the post-code system.

By Friday of a working week, after cycling three hundred miles or so, I found my bicycle had bled into my being, infecting me with its surfaces of leather and steel. Its chromium forks thrummed in sympathy with my heart rate. The cadence of my pedal strokes corresponded with my breathing. I began to feel better on the bike than off it. When I stopped cycling, when I got off the bike at the end of a week's work, the memory of the miles covered was registered in the stiffness of my legs, in the weariness of my arms, in the cramps which twitched and danced their way across my calves. The city itself persisted only as a series of brief snap-shots, stills from a film that lay inert until animated again by the flicker of pedal and wheel.

2

– Circulation –

It seemed that a pattern was beginning to emerge, having
to do with the mail and how it was delivered.
– Thomas Pynchon, *The Crying of Lot 49*

I n order to survive a week on the road, in order to
make any money at all as a courier, you need to wear
the right clothing. In the heroic era of bicycle road racing, during the first few decades of the twentieth century, riders used raw steaks slipped down their shorts
as cushions to ease the pain of bumpy roads: sacrificial
flesh to cool their seeping wounds. It was a macabre
but necessary treatment. The health of the backside is
of the utmost importance to the long-distance cyclist.
Races are won or lost over the condition of a rider's
arse. 'The cyclist's derrière,' writes Paul Fournel:

is the locus of historic dramas, of furious boils, of sneaky
swellings that alter the outcome of races. For me it's the locus
of a particular intelligible sensitivity. With my eyes closed I'm
sure I could recognise, just by sitting in the saddle, the texture
of a road long ago inscribed in me.

It's Friday morning and I'm getting ready for the day's work. I put on a woollen cycling jersey and pull on my shoes, still slightly damp from the previous day's rain. Outside, a woman throws batches of sodden bread from her balcony. Pigeons wheel in to feed. I drink a pint of milk and turn on the radio attached to the bag strap that runs like a bandoleer across my chest. I don't talk into it yet – this time is still my own – but its gentle burble of static and talk breaks the silence.

I leave my house in a daze, more body than mind. The cleats on the stiff soles of my cycling shoes clatter on the concrete. They impose a flat-footed slap and shuffle on my gait, and I'll feel awkward until I start to ride. Four days' work have taken their toll on my legs. My knees creak and click. Long-term cycling is a demonstration of Cartesian dualism. Some days feel better than others, with my legs prepared to do what's asked of them by my mind. On others they protest at every turn of the cranks and only begrudgingly respond.

My bicycle is a simple manifestation of the basic mechanics of cycling. It has a steel frame, one gear, and a single brake, like a child's drawing of a bike. Steel is the best material for comfortable daily riding. It's more flexible than aluminium, soaking up bumps in the roads, and is less liable than carbon fibre to fail catastrophically.

My bicycle is a fixed-gear track bike, meaning that there is no freewheel mechanism and thus no coasting, only the continuing turn of pedal and wheel. It's a setup designed for racing round a velodrome, and it allows you to adjust your speed with some subtlety – useful for cycling in heavy traffic, where any misjudged yank of a brake might get you rear-ended. The very first Tours de France were ridden on bicycles like this one, and the riders had to get off and flip their wheels over when they reached the tops of the mountains in order to select a higher gear for the descent. But the on-going revolutions of leg and pedal are tiring. Every inch of travel will be accounted for; every foot advanced along the tarmac will be recorded on my legs.

The story goes that track bikes were first used on the city streets by Jamaican couriers in New York, who had grown up riding them. Some fixed-gear cyclists ride without brakes and speak breathlessly about the poetry of such movement, of the way it forces you to anticipate the decisions of other road users, the way it encourages you to look into the future. They say they feel more connected with the road on such machines, but going brakeless has never really appealed to me. You get through too much tyre rubber. My handlebars are narrow and high, allowing me to slip through the smallest of gaps in the traffic and providing an upright riding position the better to survey the road around me.

I bought this bike from a man who'd loaded a van and driven around Italy buying up vintage frames from Italian cycling clubs. It was once beautiful – a sleek racehorse built for the velodromes near Treviso – but it has taken plenty of knocks over the years. The front wheel has developed a slight wobble; a memory of an encounter with a taxi door that opened on me as I raced down Savile Row in the wet and couldn't stop in time. A wheel is a delicately balanced object, held together only by the equal and sympathetic tension of the spokes, and you can always feel when it goes out of kilter. Uneven tension strains the spokes, and every so often one will pop as I ride along, so I carry a quiver of spares in my bag.

The top tube of my frame, running from saddle to handlebars, has a ding in the paintwork from where the bars swing round and bang against it when I dismount. A few years ago I replaced the down-tube after a series of collisions stressed the steel and caused it to crack beneath the lugs. I didn't paint it, and now the steel has rusted. When it rains, orange streaks of rusty water splatter against my legs. Like the ship of Theseus, it is hard to know whether this is still the same bike I began riding when I started this work. I've gone through innumerable wheel sets and handlebar grips and cranks and cogs and chainrings and chains over the years. I've killed several expensive sealed bottom brackets, quickly slain by winter's grit and salt. Only the saddle has remained the same.

Cadence. The first pedal strokes of the day. Potential energy, provided by the trade-off between the weight of my body and gravity, overcomes the inertia of my wheels and the friction of rubber on tarmac. Momentum builds. The gentle swishing that accompanied the first few revolutions becomes a faint friction-roar as the rubber of my tyres lifts itself from the dry surface of the road and falls back down again in front, over and over. Only half an inch or so of rubber is ever in contact with the road at any time. Chain is paid out in its endless loop around sprocket and chainring, matching the distance covered by the wheel precisely, revolution by revolution. There are 49 teeth on my chainring and 17 on my cog. If I pedal one hundred revolutions per minute I travel at a speed of 20 miles per hour. For every full pedal stroke I move 17 feet along the road. The mathematics of the bicycle measures the city turn by turn.

At 8.30 a.m., Old Street is clogged with other cyclists. Lycra-clad bankers head into the City on their carbon-framed racers, wobbly commuters on Boris bikes hug the gutter. Suited Brompton riders glide through the gaps. Graphic designers and web developers, bound for Soho, drift by on their track bikes, studiously ignoring everyone else. The number of cyclists on London's streets follows the seasons, mushrooming in the summer but shrinking away in winter or on rainy days when only the hardy soloists remain.

I join the peloton, attacking when I see a gap until I've moved to the front of the bunch. I cast a wide loop around a pedestrian on a zebra crossing, grabbing the side of a bus to pull myself through a gap. I weave

between the taxis that are cruising the road in search of fares. Cycling in traffic like this is an opportunistic business, part instinct and part analysis. You have to move from gap to gap, navigating the flow of traffic with the detached concentration of a boulderer addressing a climbing problem.

At the lights the exhaust of a bus blasts my feet like the warm nuzzling of some enormous dog. The aerial of my radio sticks out from the strap of my bag at an angle and extends for a few inches beyond my shoulder, functioning like a cat's whiskers, alerting me to the width of gaps as I squeeze through them. My shoulders are no wider than my handlebars, so I know that if I can fit them through then the rest of my body will follow.

Out in the streets things feel oceanic. Mist hangs over the city. Buildings, built to an industrial rather than a human scale, stand by like indifferent reefs or hulking sunken ships. Taxis shark through the lanes, darting out between the rows of cars and pulling their unpredictable U-turns. The airbrakes of buses groan like the cries of whales.

In his short story 'Waiting', the novelist and psycho-geographer Will Self describes a visionary motorbike courier, Carlos, who becomes a mystic diviner of the tarmac, able to cast calculations on the road and discern the state of traffic across the entire city as he goes. 'At every juncture where there was an opportunity for a choice,' Self writes, 'he took the right one. Carlos had not only apprehended every road, he had anticipated every alleyway, every mews, every garage forecourt and the position and synchronisation of every traffic light. He could not possibly know what he seemed to know – the only way he could have seen the route we took was from the air, and even then he would have had to have made constant trigonometric calculations to figure out the angles we seemed to have followed intuitively.' Carlos is able to assess the flow of the whole body of the city by observing its movement at any one point. 'Take me to any street, any street in London whatsoever where there is a constant traffic stream and just by looking at it I can know the state of every other road in the city. Then there's no waiting. You understand? I never have to wait.'

Cycle couriering grants access to something

resembling this secret knowledge of the city, to this sense of never having to wait. Though I'd lived in London all my life, until I began working as a courier I never quite realised how it all fits together. My experience of London had been of a fragmented, disconnected city composed of a series of separate parts, each surrounding an isolated tube station or bus stop. Because of its scale and lack of centralised plan, London has always resisted the ownership of the gaze. It's too vast to be seen from any single point; too fragmented to be reduced to a predictable series of sectors or *arrondissements*. No Haussmann has ever succeeded in standardising its layout. At street level it remains untamed, which makes it difficult to map.

Many people, even life-long Londoners, don't really know the city they live in. They have vague notions of east and west, of north and south. They associate certain areas with certain activities – work and leisure, home and away – but they are isolated from the whole by London's scale, and by those mediating technologies through which they generally encounter it: screens and maps and the public transport networks which conspire to divorce people from places. Conditioned by these ways of encountering the city, before I became a courier I had only vague notions of its topography. London had been for me an archipelago of concrete islands, but couriering drained the ocean between them, drawing the map together in my mind.

The first courier company that would give me a job without any experience was a desperate outfit based in a railway arch in Hoxton, just about clinging on amongst the graphic designers and internet entrepreneurs which have come to dominate the area. Fleetway Flyers consisted of two men who sat in their squalid office issuing edicts to a ragged band of riders through an aging Bakelite microphone. Trevor owned the operation and Frank did the controlling. Frank was an Irishman with a lilting voice, Trevor a myopic old cockney.

The yellowed, curling map of London pinned to the wall of the office was rarely consulted. Day after day the runs remained the same. Fossilised routes were trailed in greasy fingermarks across the battered *A–Z* that lived in the office, and carved into the brains of the regular riders like paths across a muddy field. For most of the day Trevor and Frank sat doing the *Sun* crossword and drinking instant coffee from Styrofoam cups which they'd slowly nibble to pieces, interrupted only by the occasional trilling of the phones. In the afternoon Trevor would go out and lose money on the horses.

My colleagues at Fleetway were a diverse bunch, but they all had their reasons for being there. Like running away to sea, or joining the circus, couriering can appeal, as it did for me, as a mild act of rebellion. Others worked the circuits because they had to. You don't need to speak very good English to be a bicycle courier, and so the workforce is composed largely of economic migrants, attracted by the lax fiscal scrutiny and flexible working hours. As long as the packages got delivered then the controllers had little interest in who did the delivering. When one courier got deported another would silently inherit his bicycle and call sign – a number used to identify a rider out on the road – only a slightly modulated accent over the radio betraying the change.

Most couriers are young, male, and slightly lost. There are a few older riders, career couriers, but most do the job only for a few years in their twenties, before thinking about exit strategies in their thirties. Many are overeducated for the job yet unwilling, for whatever reason, to commit to a regular nine-to-five existence. Some have other projects to attend to – they're writers, artists or actors – and the flexibility of the work allows them to pursue these callings on their own terms.

But the mobile nature of the workforce attracts drifters too, people unequipped or unwilling to do other kinds of work. In *Tropic Of Capricorn*, Henry Miller's account of working as a controller for the 'Cosmodemonic Telegraph Company of America' – a lightly fictionalised version of Western Union, where Miller worked for years before becoming a novelist – he describes the bulk of the messengers he employed as 'driftwood', temporary workers ready to be sacrificed on the altar of the American labour market.

We were a mixed bag at Fleetway, but most of us

were driftwood. Manuel had become a courier because he was on the run from the police in his native country and could get no other job without attracting undue attention. The work allowed him to maintain his copious and various drug addictions too, as he only had to appear sober for the few minutes he was inside buildings, face-to-face with receptionists, in order to pass. The wild-eyed stare and jittering tics he'd developed over the years could always be explained away to those he encountered on the road as the results of profound exhaustion: signatures of fatigue sympathetically awakened by the mechanisms of the city itself.

Markus had to be a courier. He was otherwise unemployable because he looked so frightening. His eyes bulged, his ham-like forearms flexed. Each of his thighs was like the belly of a foal. A fringe of ragged dreadlocks rimmed his head like a halo. The puckered kisses of numerous stab wounds ran across his torso and the varicose relief of bruise-coloured tattoos spidered over his arms and legs.

Mike had grown up on a Traveller site but had run away at sixteen and come to the city to seek his fortune. He rode a fixed-gear mountain bike with no brakes. He drank cider, and revelled in the YouTube footage of him pulling out one of his own rotten teeth with a pair of pliers. By night he organised raves on the foreshore of the Thames.

Christian Adam became a courier because it offered good opportunities for proselytising and pamphlet distribution, and because he liked the image of bringing the good news by bicycle, one pedal stroke at a time. I asked him once about his evangelical faith and he told me he believed that he was part of the elect, and that it would therefore only be right of him to offer God the chance to take his life at least five times a day. He spoke about 'the passion of the road' and the 'grace of traffic', and rode with a glow-in-the-dark rosary dangling from his saddle. Standing by while waiting for work, he'd preach the Word. No one paid him much attention. He had left his young family behind in Poland, he told me once, and sent money back each week to pay off a loan he'd taken out to repair his parents' home.

Bicycle couriering tends to attract the forgotten, people who have fallen through the cracks of the system: migrants flying under the radar; gentle, solitary alcoholics who pedal around with cans of Strongbow in their bidon holders; high-functioning smack-heads with their gap-toothed smiles and machine-gun badinage, who travel always with the animated shuffle of the addict looking for a fix. Some are merely dedicated cyclists unable to pursue a career in the professional racing peloton through lack of talent or dedication. But most are running away from something.

I became a courier not so much for economic reasons as for the other things it seemed to offer. I thought of myself as following George Orwell's lead, gaining an understanding of hard work at the coalface of capitalism in order to salve my conscience. I was beguiled by the wonderfully straightforward economies of the job. As a courier it is easy to see what, precisely, you are being paid to do: earnings are measured in miles – the distance theory of value. Carry a package from one postcode to another and you get paid accordingly. If it needs to go further or get there quickly you get paid a bit more.

Since their invention, bicycles have been used to carry messages. In Paris in the late nineteenth century men and boys on penny-farthings and velocipedes delivered cheques from bank to bank, or covered the final miles of a fledgling telegraph network, carrying messages from telegraph office to recipient. As the car came to dominate in cities the use of bicycle messengers waned slightly. But then traffic built up, and congestion slowed the car again. Nowadays, the average speed of traffic in London is the same as it was one hundred years ago – about 8 m.p.h., the speed of the horse. In the 1960s people began using bicycles to deliver packages in the city once again, and by the 1980s New York and London saw an explosion in bicycle couriers working the congested streets, competing with the other communication networks that were then emerging.

Nowadays, bicycle couriers carry everything and anything the city needs to function. Couriers carry physical objects that haven't yet been replaced by images or data streams: bundles of legal papers tied together with their jaunty pink ribbons; video tapes and DVDs from production companies to edit suites; jewellery and clothing samples from East End sweat-shops to West End PR firms; blood and urine samples from hospital to hospital; contracts from production companies to talent holed up in Primrose Hill mansions; forgotten keys or mobile phones from pubs or strip-clubs to offices; congratulatory bottles of champagne from agents to the stage-doors of west end theatres. Sometimes you deliver to famous addresses: to 10 Downing Street, where you're ushered through the gate and instructed to knock on the front door; to Tony Blair's house, where armed policemen eye you suspiciously. I once carried a box of teabags from Fortnum & Mason to Buckingham Palace.

Then there are the shady jobs, conducted on behalf of London's secret, underground economy, jobs you wouldn't want to be stopped and searched carrying. At one company I worked for I was regularly asked to carry grubby wraps of coke picked up from flat-capped dealers outside pubs and delivered to suited bankers in the City ('Don't take it to the post room,' the controllers would urge, 'he'll meet you outside'), or dodgy tickets from touts to clients. I carried envelopes stuffed with cash to pay off post-room managers in order to keep the contracts running. Other jobs were merely peculiar. One client used to send us to the Masons' supply shops on Great Queen Street, opposite the Grand High Lodge, to collect insignia and strange ritualistic objects for him: rectangular briefcases and tied aprons for delivery to anonymous suburban semis.

Sometimes couriers carry valuables. A controller once told me a story of a group of thieves who had bought themselves a radio tuned to the frequencies used by the courier companies. They'd wait on the side streets around Hatton Garden, the centre of London's jewellery district, eavesdropping on jobs being picked up on the street. When they heard of a likely sounding job they'd arrive at the pickup before the courier could, dressed in appropriate clothing, and steal the package. Controllers are still jumpy about being overheard sending out big jobs over the radio, and so any explicit discussion of the value of a package is done by mobile phone.

Now the old hands say the heyday of the cycle courier is over. Before the internet you used to make £500 a week, they say. Easy. Shuttling tapes and adcopy around London, keeping the whole monumental edifice running. The city fed on sweat, but it paid you for that sweat. In the '80s and early '90s there were maybe a thousand cycle couriers making a half decent living in London. But then the fax machines arrived, taking a chunk of that time-sensitive work, and then the Internet came along and ate into the rest. Still a few hundred couriers cling on, scraping a living alongside – or in spite of – the new networks that constantly threaten to replace them.

Nowadays couriers carry data as well, the capacity

of our bags having increased over and above the speed of the digital networks. Thirty years ago we might have carried the digital equivalent of a couple of megabytes of data in our bags. Now we can still, over short distances at any rate, carry information more quickly and cheaply than wires and fibre optic cables can. And so we carry hard drives and DVDs packed with terabytes of data, the inflation of storage capacity just about outstripping the available bandwidth of the networks.

At Fleetway my days would begin in Bunhill Fields, on the edge of the City of London. It was a good place to begin the day's work: near the office in Hoxton, equidistant from the City circuits and those of the West End. It seemed, too, like an appropriate place from which to embark on my cyclogeographic investigations of the city. Many London writers are buried here: William Blake, Daniel Defoe, John Bunyan. Other journeys have started here, some more revolutionary than others. On 15 September 1784 the balloonist Vincenzo Lunardi made the first ascent in a helium balloon in England from what's now the cricket ground of the Royal Artillery Company next door. His impatient audience, 200,000 strong, forced him to leave prematurely, without his co-pilot, and so he drifted north for 24 miles with only a cat and a dog for ballast and company before finishing his adventure at Standon Green End in Hertfordshire.

Nearly one hundred years after Lunardi, the gyroscopic miracle of the bicycle was first demonstrated to an incredulous London public just round the corner on Old Street. The writer John Mayall described the experience of witnessing this revolutionary trick of physics, in the *Ixion*, the sporting newspaper he edited:

In the early part of January 1869, I was at Spencer's Gymnasium in Old Street, St. Luke's when a foreign-looking packing-case was brought in […]. A slender young man, whom I soon came to know as Mr. Turner of Paris, followed the packing-case and superintended its opening; the gymnasium was cleared, Mr. Turner took off his coat, grasped the handles of the machine, and with a short run, to my intense surprise, vaulted on to it, and, putting his feet on the treadles, made the circuit of the room. We were some half-dozen spectators, and I shall never forget our astonishment at the sight of Mr. Turner whirling himself around the room, sitting on a bar above a pair of wheels in a line that ought, as we innocently supposed, to fall down immediately he jumped off the ground. Judge then of our surprise when, instead of stopping by tilting over on one foot, he slowly halted, and turning the front wheel diagonally, remained quite still, balancing on the two wheels.

This was the point at which, freed from the inelegant vibrations associated with the early hobbyhorses and chainless boneshakers, the bicycle proper could begin to establish itself as an efficient and practical alternative to the horse.

Inspired by the demonstration, the following day

Mayall borrowed Turner's velocipede and took it to Portland Place where, over the course of a few hours, he taught himself to ride it. 'Even nowadays the cycling novice requires plenty of room,' wrote Charles G. Harper in his account of this, the first bicycle ride to be made on London's streets, 'and as Portland Place is well known to be the widest street in London, and nearly the most secluded, it seems probable that this intrepid pioneer deliberately chose it in order to have due scope for his evolutions.' Later, after having learnt to stay upright, Mayall 'lumbered into Regent's Park, and so to the drinking fountain near the Zoological Gardens, where, in attempting to turn round, he fell over again. Mounting once more, he returned.' After a while a park-keeper came to tell him off. 'Thus early began the long warfare between Cycling and authority,' Harper notes.

Bicycles would go on to democratise transport and establish themselves in the cultural imagination as symbols of freedom and self-reliance. John Keats (himself reputed to have been born just down the road form Bunhill Fields, on the site of what is now the Globe Inn) may have called the hobbyhorse the 'nothing of the day', but only half a century later Turner's pedal-driven velocipede had proved to be immensely popular with Londoners. By 1884 Michael Mulhill's *Dictionary of Statistics* recorded 9,800 cyclists in London, thronging its parks and green spaces, wobbling down its streets and alleyways, flowing through the arteries of the Victorian city. These days about half a million journeys are made by bicycle in London every day.

For the first ten minutes of the day I would sit next to the grave of John Bunyan, smoking cigarettes while listening to crackles from the radio as the circuits warmed up. Cycle couriers live as parasites on the city – skimming a living off the top of commercial exchange – and are parasitic on its architecture, too, and on the flow of its traffic. A bicycle is only faster than a car or motorbike across town because the roads are clotted with too many vehicles.

Couriers cling on because they are able to exist in the economic and architectural edgelands, exploiting the liminal zones of the modern city. On slow days we spend a lot of time waiting around, dead time whiled away on park benches, street corners or the steps in front of buildings. Many couriers exist off the grid – living as squatters in abandoned buildings, carrying all their possessions in their enormous messenger bags, foraging for discarded food in the bins outside supermarkets. And so as a courier I became good at discovering those places where the city offers amenity. Stand-by spots, those places where we sit and wait for work, grow up around architectural quirks that create a sympathetic environment in the midst of concrete, glass and steel: a street corner close to some public toilets, a wall under the ducts that spew out warm, re-cycled air from the bowels of buildings.

While I sat with other riders waiting for work we would complain about our aching knees and tired, worn-out legs. We'd discuss the state of trade, speculat-ing about how much money everyone else was earning. We compared notes on bad controlling. We recalled injustices: being stopped by the police for running red lights at particular junctions; being sent by controllers on great schleps across the city with only one job in the bag. Most of all we would discuss the weather, pre-dicting rain with the gloomy earnestness of farmers or fishermen, dreading the dry heat that wore us out dur-ing the summer.

During quiet periods we would memorialise the city too, discussing our favourite streets and the perfect runs we'd made along them, hymning serendipitous formations of tarmac, those sweet-spots of camber and incline we had discovered hidden in the grid. We would go misty-eyed over postcodes that had some special sig-nificance for us. We compared notes on our bicycles, discussing the merits of different frame materials and gear ratios. We listed road names and their postcodes, describing our journeys in shorthand, proudly display-ing our knowledge of the city to each other.

Frank, my controller at Fleetway, was an Ahab-like savant who ran the circuit as a benign dictator-ship. We let him because he was a good controller, able to keep track of things better than any of his riders, remembering where you were and how many jobs you had on board with an uncanny precision, better than you did yourself. Frank was an ex-cabbie, and the Knowledge swamped his brain. He had been expelled from school at fourteen for stealing mopeds, he once told me, and spent his teenage years as a scholar of the city: joyriding cars and motorbikes down its alleyways and culs-de-sac, learning every back road and aerial walkway, every park and passage and byway and rat-run. He used this mental armoury first to evade the police and later, more legitimately, as a taxi driver. But after a few years on the road he realised that he preferred his mental map of the city to the real thing, and so he retreated to the office to live in it at one remove, traversing London vicariously in his imagination.

Frank worked where he was needed, dodging round the office between the four bike radio channels. With two teams of riders – Bravo and Delta – each divided between the east and the west, London was cleaved into two hemispheres like an enormous brain, the corpus callosum an imaginary line running down Kingsway. Frank was able to keep track of every job and the location of every bike with barely a mistake made. It was a formidable task. There were about forty bicycle couriers at Fleetway, each pushing out twenty or so jobs a day, but Frank rarely forgot the location of any of his riders, remembering dockets from days, weeks, past. Signatures were lodged in his brain as firmly as they were on paper or in the computer. He wielded his riders like a strategist mapping a battle.

When things went well, the network of jobs throbbing into life, the orbits of his riders coming together as a piece of complicated choreography, you could hear the excitement in his voice. 'Am I good, am I good?' he would call out across the airwaves as he described a particularly satisfying rhomboid onto the West End.

Controllers have the bingo-caller's efficacy, the get-there-before-you-can vocal speed of auctioneers. The jobs themselves go out in code, skeletal details declaimed as call-and-response:

'One-nine?'
'This is one-nine.'
'Direct at 78 Newman Street.'
'Roj.'
'Thirty-six?'
'Three-six.'
'Three-six, in the middle yet?'
A pause.
'Ah. Silence is golden'
'Six-four.'
'Come again who's calling?'
'Six-four.'
'Six-four?'
'On the bounce from west fifteen.'
'OK, keep coming, keep coming.'
'Nine-six?'
'Nine-six.'

'One on the island for you, going west one.'
'Roger.'

The jobs went out in these Beckettian sentences, skeletal descriptions of the day's work. The busyness of the day was measured out in the panic of the controllers' voices, boredom or fatigue or mutiny echoed in riders' responses.

On an open circuit, when you can hear everyone else speaking, the radio functions as a portal, opening sonic windows across the city. The whine of a police siren asserts itself in the background whilst a rider responds to a call; the ambient chatter of other couriers betrays one who has claimed to have a puncture and is catching a few minutes rest with company. Someone once told me a harrowing story about listening over the radio to a colleague who had been hit by a lorry. After the crash and the silence, a voice announced, 'I'm here, I'm alive: I'm trapped under an HGV.'

The radio eliminates time and distance, offering a rebuke to the tardy material procession of the city's other traffic. After a while you come to know the voices of controllers and other riders as intimately as you do your own. Some of them I'm sure I never met, but I invented potted biographies of them based on their accents, on their seeming enthusiasms and their radio manners. Seven-three, a polite and deferential Brazilian who called Frank 'sir' and 'boss' and never raised his voice; nine-one, an irascible New Zealander who was always threatening to go home early; six-three, a girl whose name I never learned, who spoke softly and thoughtfully, measuring each word before it was deployed; nine-nine, a verbose Welshman so well-spoken he could easily have been a continuity announcer on Radio Four.

My London was soundtracked by this chorus of disembodied voices floating over the airwaves, tipping each other off about speed traps and traffic snarl-ups: a private pirate station broadcasting its unofficial communiqués across the city. Sometimes I would turn on the radio even when I wasn't at work and sit listening to the litany of jobs as I wrote, idly imagining the journeys it called forth.

3

– Cartesian Centaurs –

Consider the cyclist as he passes, the supreme specialist,
transfiguring that act of moving from place to place which is
itself the sentient body's supreme specialty. He is the term of
locomotive evolution from slugs and creeping things.
– Hugh Kenner, *Samuel Beckett*

B icycle couriering is difficult, dangerous work. Couriers are paid for piecework and employed as self-employed subcontractors, meaning there's no sick pay, no employment protection, no pension scheme. You earn only what you ride for. If you're injured while working your employers have no obligation to you. Apart from the assistance of the London Courier Emergency Fund – a grass-roots organisation run by couriers that pays out small amounts to riders injured on the job – you're on your own.

Physically, the work is grindingly difficult. On an average day you'll cycle sixty to one hundred miles, deliver twenty or so packages, and earn maybe three pounds per package. On a good day you'll break £100. On a fixed-gear bike like mine, with a gearing of 49/17, that amounts to around 29,000 complete pedal revolutions per day. On an average day you'll earn 0.003p for each turn of the cranks. On slow days you often earn far less than minimum wage. You're largely ignored, if not disdained, by the people you work for. Like other dangerous work it fosters a strong sense of community, an informal support network focused on races, drinking, and listening to interminable stories about bad controlling or those one-off, impossibly lucrative jobs and satisfying runs.

I had a choice, of course, when many people don't, but for me the sheer joy of being physically tired at the end of a day's work was a revelation. In *The Soul of London,* Ford Madox Ford described labour in London as divided fairly equally between that of the mind and that of the body. 'Workers in London,' he wrote, 'divide themselves, roughly, into those who sell the labour of their bodies and those who sell their attentions. You see men in the streets digging trenches, pulling stout wires out of square holes in pavements, pecking away among greasy vapours at layers of asphalt, scattering shovelfuls of crushed gravel under the hoofs of slipping horses and under the crunching tyres of wheels. If walls would fall out of offices you would see paler men and women adding up the records of money paid to these others. That, with infinite variations, is work in London.'

Since Ford's time the balance has altered, and labour in London, as in many post-industrial cities, has become predominantly cerebral or service-based. For me couriering felt like one of the few ways left in the city to work with my body. Through cycling miles and miles each day I got to know it alongside the city. I learned how much food and water it needed to run smoothly, how it performed in the heat or in the rain. I learned its limits, alongside those of London.

Increasingly, the lives of our bodies have become disciplined, made to conform to the stranglehold of nine-to-five existence. One of the reasons walking has become such a popular topic for writers is that physical exertion is nowadays often isolated from everyday being. Mostly, the needs of our bodies are allowed to announce themselves only at prearranged times: during the regularly scheduled run or gym appointment. In *Wanderlust* Rebecca Solnit argues that people have forgotten about their bodies, forgotten that they are more than mere vehicles for minds, passive vessels to be inhabited by our all-important egos. We have forgotten that our bodies 'could be adequate to the challenges that face them and a pleasure to use,' she writes; we 'perceive and imagine [our] bodies as essentially passive, a treasure or a burden but not a tool for work and travel.' What Solnit calls the 'vital body in action' has been largely misplaced in post-industrial society: lost to a world of digital distraction or annexed to the contained and constraining fields of 'work' and 'play'. A Heideggerian notion of being-in-the-world has been replaced with the feeling that we experience reality only through and within a variety of tightly controlled spaces: cars, cubicles, and offices.

Couriering reminded me about the existence of

my body. Daily I felt the delicious burn of muscles, the faintness of pure hunger and sugar crashes – 'meeting', as racing cyclists put it, 'the man with the hammer' – and the deep pleasure of slaking real thirst. After a year on the road couriering ceased to feel like a temporary job, a stop-gap between university courses and some still unknown career, and became all-consuming. I got sucked in.

For most of the twentieth century the bicycle was explicitly associated with work. The on-yer-bikism of Norman Tebbit, the conservative MP who in the 1980s advised the unemployed to get on their bikes to find work, merely reflected a more deep-seated association between the self-propelled movement of cycling and labour: of pedalling to work *as* work. It was partly for this reason that, at the turn of the century, English socialists seized on the bicycle as a vehicle for political agitation. The *Clarion*, a left wing newspaper founded in 1891, started life as a socialist cycling club, and later its members would deliver the paper by bicycle. In Italy, communists founded a group called the 'Red Cyclists' to campaign for 'cheap bikes for the working classes', while manufacturers tried to cash in on the socialist revolution of cycling by producing a bicycle tyre branded the 'Karl Marx'. For the Red Cyclists, writes the historian John Foot, the symbolism was obvious: 'to pedal was to work. The bike was the "vehicle of the poor" and the "ally of their effort."'

In the professional peloton of the heroic era of bicycle racing, too, the bicycle represented labour. Professional cyclists still aren't paid a great deal, especially those who aren't famous, but before the Second World War a bicycle race represented an opportunity: a chance for poor farm hands to break away from the constraints of their lives. 'A racing cyclist, at least in the old days,' writes Foot 'was a worker: one who did, and was paid a wage based on the races they won, on how well they performed.' Much like couriering, racing was paid as piecework. In the early years of road cycling, before doping was made illegal, before the trade teams and the sponsored coddling, before the hyper-tactical machinations of the contemporary sport, 'cyclists were individuals battling against the elements and the limits imposed by their own bodies,' writes Foot. Racing itself was heavily politicised. For those on the left of the political spectrum – both writers and riders – the peloton was interpreted as a socialist utopia, a field of common endeavour within which racers could help each other out or show solidarity by neutralising the race, or providing aerodynamic cover for their stars. For the right the race represented the triumph of individual exceptionalism.

In Luigi Bartolini's 1946 novel *Bicycle Thieves*, made into a film in 1948 by Vittorio De Sica, the bicycle becomes a symbol of escape from the poverty of post-war Italy. A poor unemployed man named Antonio is offered a job delivering and putting up posters around Rome. The job stipulates that he must provide his own bicycle, and so his wife Maria sells her best bed linen to reclaim the bike Antonio has previously pawned. On his first day of work his bicycle is stolen from under his nose and, accompanied by his son Bruno, Antonio embarks on a kind of cyclogeographic tour of Rome's less salubrious quarters to reclaim it.

The film is a quest narrative. Antonio and Bruno follow strangers through the crowds, they search for parts of his bicycle at Piazza Vittorio market, where dealers spread their deconstructed machines in front of them like piles of fruit. They find a bicycle that they think is Antonio's and alert a passing policeman, but the serial numbers don't match. They visit a working-man's chapel and are forced to endure a sermon before continuing their search. At one point they give up all hope of finding the bike and, drunk with despair, Antonio spends the last of his money on a slap-up lunch in an up-market trattoria. Eventually, desperate to keep the job which was to provide an escape from poverty, Antonio himself becomes a bicycle thief. He is quickly apprehended, but the man whose bicycle he has stolen notices Bruno and, in a moment of compassion, pardons Antonio, who is left to walk home forlornly with his son. *Bicycle Thieves* is about the desperations of poverty, but it is also a meditation on the bicycle as a vehicle for self-determination through work. It's a film I often thought about as I cycled around the city.

The association of the bicycle with labour during the mid-twentieth century was partly born of its curious hybridity as a machine. Cyclists' bodies are subdued to their instruments, and riding another person's bike often feels intensely alien. It is a cliché that the bike, of all tools, can become an extension of the body, but it is nonetheless true for that. After a while on the road you begin to worry about your bike as though it is a part of you. Anxiously you check the small areola of rust surrounding the hole at the bottom of the chromed seat stays; the notch in the headset giving your steering a slight bias; the creak of the wheel caused by a cracked spoke.

Many writers have reflected on the neatness of the Cartesian metaphor of bicycle and rider as body and mind, as dualist parts of a unified whole. At the dawn of the cycling era the strange logic of the bicycle – the way in which cycling creates a prosthetic relation between person and machine – was seized upon in particular by Futurist and modernist writers and artists, invested as they were in the triumph of the mechanical over the mental, or at least, in a future where human inadequacies could be engineered away by the application of reason. For these writers the conceit was obvious: people didn't ride bicycles, bicycles rode people. The bike was a symbol of Man multiplied by machine.

In one of his Futurist manifestoes F. T. Marinetti associated the bicycle with other emerging technologies, prophesying the deranging stimulants of the mechanical age:

Those people who today make use of the telegraph, the telephone, the phonograph, the train, the bicycle, the motorcycle, the automobile, the ocean liner, the dirigible, the aeroplane, the cinema, the great newspaper (synthesis of a day in the world's life) do not realise that these various means of communication, transportation and information have a decisive influence on their psyches.

Like Marinetti, the artist Fernand Léger interpreted the act of cycling as the coming together of body and machine, but also as a form of art. 'A bicycle operates in the realm of light,' he wrote, 'it takes control of legs, arms and body, which move on it, by it and under it. Rounded thighs become pistons, which rise or fall, fast or slow.' The threat to autonomy associated with industrialised labour was prefigured by the threat to the individual will demonstrated by the bicycle.

The French playwright and poet Alfred Jarry, founder of the playfully counter-intuitive discipline of 'Pataphysics' – which he defined as 'the science of imaginary solutions' – called the bicycle Man's 'external skeleton', and rode a state-of-the-art Clement machine running the impossibly high gear ratio of 36/9, so that his wheels revolved four times for every turn of his pedals.

Jarry saw the bicycle as the epitome of Pataphysical technology. As he rode around Paris he would let off a pair of pistols to deter attacking dogs, and he later scandalised society by wearing his cycling outfit to the funeral of the poet Stéphane Mallarmé. When he died Jarry left an unpaid bill for a bicycle which would contribute to the bankruptcy of his sister. She died soon after.

Cycling, and the image of mechanised hybridity it provided, was central to Jarry's writing. In his short story 'The Crucifixion Considered as an Uphill Bicycle Race' he rewrote the passion of the Christ in the breathless high style of newspaper reports of the newly inaugurated bicycle races which were then sweeping France:

Jesus got away to a good start. In those days, according to the excellent sports commentator St. Matthew, it was customary to flagellate the sprinters at the start the way a coachman whips his horses. The whip both stimulates and gives a hygienic massage. Jesus, then, got off in good form, but he had a flat right away. A bed of thorns punctured the whole circumference of his front tyre.

Five years before his death, Jarry wrote his last novel, *The Supermale*. In it he described a 10,000-mile race between a group of cyclists and a train, the riders fuelled by a mysterious 'perpetual motion food' made up of strychnine and alcohol. One rider dies but is contractually obliged to finish the race. For Jarry bicycle and body formed a self-sustaining system: the legs were massaged by the act of pedalling; the body self-lubricated as sweat gathered between the thighs:

Alfred Jarry riding in Paris. His wheels revolved four times
for every turn of his pedals.

Complex nervous and muscular systems enjoy absolute rest, it
seems to me, while their 'counterpart' works. We know that,
for a bicyclist, each leg in turn rests, and even benefits from a
massage that is automatic, and as restorative as any embroca-
tion, while the other leg is doing the work.

Bound by metal rods to their machines, the five-
man crew cycle from Paris to Asia paced by flying
machines, reaching speeds of 300 kilometres an hour.
The Supermale pointed towards a disturbing future in
which the body would be utterly dehumanised by the
bicycle, enslaved by the machines that had once prom-
ised freedom.

Samuel Beckett too was obsessed with the deranged

metaphysics of cycling, with the philosophical lessons that could be learnt from the saddle. According to the critic Hugh Kenner, Godot himself was an avatar for 'Monsieur Godeau', a French national champion cyclist who typified 'Cartesian man in excelsis'. For Beckett the bicycle represented the triumph of what Kenner calls 'the simple machines' – lever, pulley, gear – over man in a state of nature:

To consider the endless perfection of the chain, the links forever settling about the cogs, is a perpetual pleasure; to reflect that a specified link is alternately stationary with respect to the sprocket, then in motion with respect to the same sprocket, without hiatus between these conditions, is to entertain the sort of soothing mystery which [. . .] you can study all your life and not understand. The wheels are a miracle; the contraption moves on air, sustained by a network of wires in tension not against gravity but against one another.

Many of Beckett's characters are dependent on the material crutch of their bicycles for support. In *More Pricks than Kicks*, Belacqua Shuah forgoes his human companion when he spots a bicycle lying in a field, before stealing it, lying down in the grass with it, and attempting to make love to it. When Molloy is separated from his bicycle he breaks down, starts staggering around in circles and eventually becomes unable to walk, so pulls himself along on his belly using his crutches before rolling into a ditch. In *Watt*, the eponymous character dreams of bicycles as he enters the house of Knott. Beckett's bikes, like Jarry's, are often sinister objects. In *Mercier and Camier* he wrote 'the bicycle is a great good. But it can turn nasty, if ill employed.' His prose evokes the bicycle at the level of the sentence too, filled as it is with its cyclical rhythms: those emergent, flowing sentences animated by short-term repetitions: a ratchet-prose ramping up momentum and significance with each turn of the cranks.

Beckett's fellow Irish author Flann O'Brien was an equally visionary cyclist-mystic. In the cyclical hell of *The Third Policeman* he documented the curious psycho-sexual relationship that could develop between people and bicycles from within the confines of a profoundly strange detective novel. According to O'Brien's 'Atomic Theory', over time cyclists begin to merge with their machines due to the exchange of atoms between the two. The unnamed narrator of *The Third Policeman* communes with his bike, becoming one with it as they traverse the bad roads of the purgatorial Parish:

How can I convey the perfection of my comfort on the bicycle, the completeness of my union with her, the sweet responses she gave me at every particle of her frame? I felt that I had known her for many years and that she had known me and that we understood each other utterly [...] I passed my hand with unintended tenderness – sensuously indeed – across the saddle [...] It was a gentle saddle yet calm and courageous

[...] Her saddle seemed to spread invitingly into the most enchanting of all seats while her two handlebars, floating finely with the wild grace of alighting wings, beckoned to me to lend my mastery for free and joyful journeyings, the lightest of light running in the company of the swift ground to safe havens far away, the whir of the true front wheel in my ear as it spun perfectly beneath my clear eye and the strong fine back wheel with unadmired industry raising gently dust on the dry roads. How desirable her seat was, how charming the invitation of her slim encircling handlebars, how unaccountably competent and reassuring her pump resting warmly against her rear thigh.

In O'Brien's novel the bicycle is given volition, becoming a character in its own right. With his 'Atomic Theory' O'Brien argued (with the pub-bore's grasp of particle physics) that the constant exchange of atoms between Man and bicycle would eventually affect the psychology of each. And the process wasn't just one way. Not only do bikes in *The Third Policeman* become endowed with humanity, humanity takes on a latent bicyclosity. Cyclists begin to sleep in corridors propped up against walls on one elbow. At rest they stand with one foot on the curb and one in the gutter. Bicycles begin to steal from pantries: crumbs and tyre marks betraying this nocturnal activity. There are hints of more sinister activity, of bicycle rapes and murders. 'Of course there are other things connected with ladies and ladies' bicycles that I will mention to you separately some time,' reports Sergeant Pluck, the friendliest of the three titular policemen, 'but the man-charged bicycle is a phenomenon of great charm and intensity and a very dangerous article.'

I wanted to talk to someone about the long-term effects of couriering, about what it felt like to do the job for a decade or more, to think about it not as a stop-gap but as a career, or a calling of some kind. I wanted to know what couriers do when they retire. And so I sought out someone who'd been on the road for a while and got out without succumbing to the dark predictions of O'Brien's Atomic Theory of cycling.

'Buffalo' Bill Chidley is a messengers' messenger. He started working as a courier in the early '80s, 'when you could make real money on the road', and when a fledgling courier sub-culture – all dreadlocks, tattoos, and tiny cycling hats – was beginning to emerge. The bicycle courier became a recognisable social type in the '80s, Bill recalls, immortalised in the children's TV show *Streetwise* and then, later, as 'Tyres', the rave-haunted courier in the sitcom *Spaced*. Bill retired after a decade in the saddle, and now works as a controller and edits *Moving Target*, a bicycle messenger fanzine. He still looks like a courier. Keys jangle from his belt. He wears a huge bag, jeans rolled at the ankle and clip-in cycling shoes. Journalists seek him out for comment on the London cycling scene. Couriers doff their caps as he passes them in the street. I knew him as a controller, and met up with him to ask about the origins of London bicycle couriering, and about what happens when you give up the job.

We met in a pub in Islington filled with a few couriers and controllers reminiscing about their time on the road. Most of them said they had become controllers because they'd been couriers and didn't know what to do when their knees gave out, or when the work began to feel too mind-numbingly futile to continue. One of the older riders drinking with them, Mike, told me he'd recently given up couriering because he was waiting for an operation on his arthritic knees. He missed the job, he said, but was keeping himself busy as a dog walker, trying to work out what to do next. He said he'd probably get back in the saddle once he'd had the operation. He couldn't think of what else to do.

Like most controllers, Bill talks with fondness and nostalgia about the job. He missed the money, the freedom, and the fact that as a courier you're paid to ride your bike for a living. Most of all he missed the City, he told me, 'I hate the City police, but I love the City.' He misses knowing London in that intimate way that is the privilege of the courier. He knew it these days on screen, or from the pages of the *A–Z*. 'I still reckon that, apart from the people who are actually doing the Knowledge, couriers know the city best,' he said.

The first recognisable bicycle courier companies in London emerged in the '80s, Bill told me. Before that minicab companies touted for whatever business there was, and the industry was mainly controlled by gangsters. 'You get a lot of talk about the cab wars in the '70s,' Bill said, 'where cab drivers from different firms fought for business. I heard talk of people going over and taking shotguns to taxi ranks. There used to be a company that trained couriers, and they traced the birth of modern couriers to the postal strike of '74. But black cabs were being used to move stuff around before then. They talk about soldiers and prostitutes as the oldest jobs. I would put messengers before them.'

I asked him if working conditions had got worse since he first started the job, if couriers earn less money these days. He said they had and they do. 'It's not like when I was on the road, in the '80s. Then *everything* needed to be sent physically. We were delivering tapes to radio stations, to TV stations. Display ad copy to Fleet Street.' When I asked him why he thinks couriers have managed to cling on against a backdrop of technological change he stressed the human component of the business. 'It's not so much that we're quicker than the internet', Bill said, 'there's also a question of security. If you don't actually have a physical private cable and you have something sensitive to send across town you need to use a courier. When they were filming *Lord of the Rings* I heard they had a private cable that came out at Pinewood. If they needed to do something with it in Soho, they weren't going to send that over the Internet. They had a private cable, hard-wired in. Nowadays we're moving hard drives around too. When they cut it really fine, then we end up moving the hard drives to the cinemas to screen the films.'

Bill's retired to the office now, away from the wind and the rain, from the weather and the city. He makes his money sending other riders to jobs. 'What do you make on us? Double?' I asked him. 'No, generally not. If we've got a vanilla job, where there's no discount, then we're making double, yeah. But there are so few of them. As a courier you're just above cleaners and just below security in the pecking order. We're an office service, so we'll tender. We'll go in and the opening gambit of our salespeople will be "Here are our prices, and today we're offering ten per cent off." Everything is negotiable, but the clients have to ask us first. Desperate companies drive the prices down for everyone. "Whatever they're doing it for we'll do it for less."'

We spoke about knowing London, about the uniqueness of the city experienced from the saddle. 'I learned London, more or less, from the tube map,' Bill said. 'You've got all these lines, and all this blank space in between. You've got this white space, and on a bike you fill in the gaps. I was born in London. But it's only when you look at the map, and you can see the railway lines, the river, that you realise how it all works. If you take somewhere like Fulham, it's actually an island. You've got the A4 across the top; you've got the river, and then these developments. Planning is supposed to make the city legible, but it doesn't.' As a controller you only really get to know the places in which your clients are based, he said. 'Some guys have been on the road for ten years and still only know Soho. Riders from my company used to have this reputation: if someone saw you east of Kingsway they'd say "The West End's that way, are you lost or something?"'

Now Bill lives through his maps, on the screen and through the radio. 'If I actually go out now and ride around, I get lost. As a courier I got bored riding round in London because by the end I couldn't get lost; you know where everything is. I went through a phase where I deliberately tried to get lost, because London's so big that the idea of knowing where you are all the time is so overwhelming. But when you arrive at a point where you can't get lost it becomes boring. Now I go out and the physical structure of the city has changed quite a bit. So it's become interesting again. But I still think that, even though I've been off the road twelve years, my knowledge is better now. I'm constantly looking at a map. Always looking at a map.'

Couriering was attractive to me, as it was to Bill, because it was easy to know you weren't exploiting anyone when you were the one being exploited. The market place is brutally efficient. Unionisation has proved almost impossible in an industry so depend-ent on migrant labour. Whole fleets are sacked and replaced overnight. 'There were several attempts to un-ionise in the '80s,' Bill said, 'but you could never push it over the line. Partly because there was always this kind of "we don't need a union" feeling. People were like "we're professional couriers", but now they're on minimum wage. The companies have managed to pit all the couriers against each other. As a controller I see the other side of it. If I can't cover a job I'm fucked. It only works if I can persuade you to do the job – come on, you know, do this for me. What I need is for everyone to help each other and trust that it'll work out.'

I asked Bill if he missed the work. 'Yeah, every day. What I miss is being outside. I ride to work and then I sit indoors. What I always miss is the sky. That's what I would be constantly looking at. You're always looking at it and asking is it going to rain? That's what I miss the most. Mostly London's weather is mediocre, but it changes. Don't like the weather now? Just wait half an hour. A new front will roll in.'

Finally we talked about leaving the job, about how to get out. It seems tricky for many. Maybe couriering makes you sad or maybe it attracts sad people to it – the endorphins generated by exercise providing a form of subtle self-medication – but it's true that many couriers have a touch of melancholia about them. Despite the dangers, in the seven years since I first began riding a bike for a living in London I have known more couriers to have committed suicide than to have died on the road. The isolation of the job can exacerbate despair and depression. The lack of structure, each day drifting into the next, becoming a never-ending cycle with no apparent way out, eats away at you after a while.

Career-couriers can easily succumb to the repetitiveness. Denied the enforced daily contact of office work, you can easily slip through the social bonds of the road to exist in a solipsistic vacuum. Then you become an eternal observer, your only social interaction coming from the brief and cursory points of contact with people at pick up and delivery, and the disembodied presence of the controller on the radio. It is easy to lose touch with things.

A few years ago I heard that a courier had committed suicide after having been stopped for running a red light. The cursory name check the police ran revealed an unpaid debt in Poland and a one-year prison sentence passed in absentia. Faced with deportation, with the loss of a life struggled for and cultivated into stability, he killed himself. He left behind his girlfriend and their young daughter.

London writers have always been drawn to the idea of hard work in a city that seems ever more dependent on brainwork. As manual labour in the city has declined, so writers have become interested in cataloguing and recording the work of the body. By George Orwell's time there was already, he wrote, a 'sort of fetish of manual work' abroad in the city:

We see a man cutting down a tree, and we make sure that he is filling a social need, just because he uses his muscles; it does not occur to us that he may only be cutting down a beautiful tree to make room for a hideous statue.

Much London writing has been obsessed with the secret history of working places, with the stories of those labouring shades who once walked and lived and worked in them. Often this interest was based on hands-on experience. Charles Dickens worked in a blacking factory as a child, a period in his life he remained deeply ashamed of. In *London Labour and the London Poor* Henry Mayhew outlined a fine-grained typology of work in the city, identifying the various castes of workers who used to keep London functioning: the mudlarks, costermongers, scavengers, and 'wandering tribes' who plied their trades on the streets of the city. In distinguishing the 'wanderers and the settlers', Mayhew wrote, 'the nomad is then distinguished from the civilised man by his repugnance to regular and continuous labour – by his want of providence in laying up a store for the future – by his inability to perceive consequences ever so slightly removed from immediate apprehension – by his passion for stupefying herbs and roots and, where possible, for intoxicating fermented liquors – by his extraordinary powers of enduring privation – by his comparative insensibility to pain.' It is a fair description of the cycle courier.

More recently, in the work of authors like Iain Sinclair, Peter Ackroyd and Rachel Lichtenstein, the idea of work as a part of the identity of urban space still seems to be central. Yet the impulse to account for this lost labour is in some respects an attempt to address the new blandness that lies at the heart of the contemporary city, with its economy dominated by service industry jobs. The labour-fetishism of much London writing has itself been diagnosed as the nostalgic result of the decline of manual labour in the city, and of the architecture associated with it: with the docks and the factories which were once London's biggest employers. In *London from Punk to Blair* Phil Baker argues that the notion of a secret city, lying parallel to the one most of us know, has always inspired London writers, but that:

[the] value of the urban secret changes from era to era. The great secret of the nineteenth century was the extent of poverty and degradation, giving rise to revelatory books such as William Booth's *In Darkest London* (1880). But by the end of the hyper-transparent late twentieth century, the secret was positive, and it was desired as never before. This desire for secret places relates to perennial fantasies of places 'off the map', like De Quincey's London *terrae incognitae,* and of liminal zones and glimpsed paradises – in the fictions of Alain-Fournier, H. G. Wells and Arthur Machen, for example – but it gains a new, belated urgency in over-developed, over-exposed millennial London.

The writer James Heartfield argues that the manual labourer now forms part of a secret lost race of 'troglodytes' that haunt the contemporary city 'cleared away in the transformation of London into a city dedicated primarily to business services and retail'. Such nostalgia is symptomatic of a larger cultural project, represented in the work-porn of television programmes such as *Deadliest Catch* and *Trawlermen*, documenting hard work and its associated dangers for our voyeuristic pleasure.

Now cycle couriering too is implicated in this decline, and is increasingly seen as a dying trade. The narrative is familiar to all couriers, whether they subscribe to it or not. Since the advent of fax and email couriers have been living at the end of days. The bike, once the 'friend of the poor' and the 'ally of their effort' is losing its proletarian edge. It has been re-appropriated, not as a tool for work but as a vehicle for leisure.

Of course, regardless of the politics, everyone *should* be cycling more, and driving less. The notion that cycling is or should be the preserve of a dwindling and 'authentic' courier crowd, let alone that of the Critical Mass riders, naked cyclists and bikepunks who see each revolution of the wheel as one more turn towards the greater revolution, is as alienating as it is wrong-headed. But on the final reckoning bike politics doesn't amount to much of anything. The fact is that most working people still prefer the underground. The cult of simplicity surrounding cycling has corresponded exactly to the decline of public infrastructure that most people use to get to work. Indeed in most cities the bicycle selfishly profits from this decline, gaining an advantage as traffic snarls up and trains fill up.

The central paradox of the labour of cycle courier-ing, therefore, is its strangely oppressive freedom. Many couriers revel in the fact that they can come and go as they please, that they work alone in the city on their own terms, that they can wear what they like and drink, smoke and take drugs all day without getting sacked. In reality of course you're the lowest in the economic food chain - capitalism's foot-soldiers, paid to pass the parcel around a massive financial circuit. And yet still the meteoric rise of the bicycle, reclaimed not as a tool of work but of leisure, continues. In an age of austerity, the underground systems of London and New York are literally grinding towards collapse. Meanwhile for a politician eager for popularity, nothing is easier than taking a can of paint and siphoning off a portion of tarmac for a bike lane. The class of people this pleases is small but increasingly vocal, highly visible in parts of the city where they were once scarce and oblivious to what was once a truth: increased cycling is a sign of decreased employment. When a bike shop appears in a depressed neighbourhood, you can be sure it's on the verge of gentrification.

Where I live in east London, the bicycle shop has become a destination in itself. Boutique bike shops serve coffee and cake whilst the mechanics, stars of the show, fix bicycles in the middle of the room while everyone watches. The nostalgia can also be seen in the bikes people choose to ride. In the '90s, Bill tells me, most couriers rode fat-tubed mountain bikes bristling with gears. Now there's been a turn towards the simple honesty of the fixed-gear track bicycle, with its single gear, its perpetually revolving pedals, its decent and uncluttered lack of brakes. Leather saddles riveted together with copper pins adorn these simple machines. People carry waxed cotton saddlebags. Lycra is banished to the lower layers. Out on the streets faux-couriers, dressed the part, cruise around on spotless steel track bikes, carrying enormous single-strap bags and wearing their bonsai cycling caps. But their bags are empty. They carry no radios. They wear the bottoms of their trousers rolled.

4

– Race –

The racer sets out, alone; he will ride as fast as possible
every second, as if there were nothing in the world but time
and himself. He never *feels* his victory.
— Roland Barthes, *What is Sport?*

On his last day of work my brother, who also
worked as a bicycle courier, organised a race.
Courier races, known as alleycats, usually consist of
straightforward if manic runs across the city. An anar-
chic peloton will gather at some anonymous starting
point before the riders commence on a mad dash from
checkpoint to checkpoint, crashing through the traffic
as a wave of rubber and steel. It's a fairly antisocial pursuit. Alleycats are parodies of the courier's day-job, ritualistic recreations of working journeys. They are utterly
devoid of purpose. Sometimes alleycats are organised
around a theme. Sometimes there are prizes, but mostly
you compete for reputation. Racers collect spoke cards
commemorating races they have completed in, which
they wear as trophies stuck between their spokes.

When I first became a courier, most of these
races began at the Foundry, a punky, ramshackle pub
on Great Eastern Street. The Foundry was a bastion

of cheap booze and anarcho-aestheticism set in the heart of Shoreditch, and was for a long time the last outpost of the underground in an area that had long ago lost its battle against gentrification. In its previous life the building had been a bank, and the vault was later used to stage exhibitions. Layers of graffiti covered every inch of the toilets. By night avant-garde jazz bands twanged their makeshift instruments in the gloom. Couriers tested the tolerance of the landlords by smuggling in their own cans of beer, but they were never barred.

My brother's race was different to the average alley-cat. It was designed as an urban steeplechase with a fox-hunt theme. He strapped a huge bottle to his back containing a few gallons of paint, with a pipe running down the frame of his bicycle, terminating in a small tap. He attached a fox's tail to one of his belt loops. At the start of the race he opened the tap and the paint started to flow as he pedalled off into the traffic, a line of white glistening on the tarmac in his wake. After a few minutes I released the racers – a pack of bicycling-hounds – with a blast of horns. The race was on.

We followed the paint that lay in a splattered line on the tarmac, competing with the other street markings and tracing a ghostly outline of my brother's journey. Like a paint-walk by the Belgian artist Francis Alÿs, the drips and splashes wrote the race onto the street. It recorded the positions of cars and buses as they had been a few minutes earlier, swerving erratically around now non-existent obstructions. It registered the ghostly outlines of the lines of traffic idling at the lights; elongated, swooping curves as my brother had cut between moving cars. It recorded his speed also. There were larger spaces between the splatters when he'd gone faster, smaller ones as he'd slowed down.

At one junction the line of paint led onto the pavement, across some blue duckboards and dropped back onto the road. Some racers followed the route blindly. Other, cannier riders spotted the line continuing further up the road and carried straight on, avoiding the now pointless detour. The hounds whooped and cheered. One fell off his bike and was left behind. Like a manic pied-piper, my brother led the pack of cyclists around the East End of London, through kissing gates, across parks and across industrial wasteland, over the shifting pavé of old cobbled streets and down the dark tunnels that run under the railway lines around Brick Lane.

After a while the splashes became irregular. The paint was running out, or the pipe was blocking up. As the pack crossed Bethnal Green Road for the second time we spotted a big splatter of paint in the gutter. My brother had slipped on a drain cover and buckled both his wheels. The race was over, and the riders skulked back to the pub. The white line can still be made out here and there on the roads around Brick Lane, a faint memorial to the route.

Around the same time I started couriering I became obsessed with bicycle road racing. I wasn't so much interested in the modern sport, in the world of carbon, titanium and doping scandals, but in stories from the dawn of bike racing in the early twentieth century, when riders were responsible for their own repairs and the only rules about doping were that drugs would not be supplied by the organisers.

In these races the image of the rider's body as a machine reached its apogee. Doping was rife. Early riders of the Tour used alcohol and ethanol to dull the pain of pushing their bodies to breaking point. In the six-day track races which were popular from the 1890s to the 1920s – races that wore riders down to inhuman lumps of twitching muscle – seconds used strychnine to tighten muscles, nitro-glycerine to terrify their rider's hearts into pushing on. Later amphetamine and cocaine tinctures became prevalent. In 1924 the cyclist Henri Pélissier gave an interview in which he described the regime he and his fellow riders underwent during big races:

cocaine for the eyes, chloroform for the gums [...] and do you want to see the pills? We ride on dynamite. When the mud is washed off us, we are as white as sheets. We are drained by diarrhoea. We dance jigs in our bedroom instead of sleeping. Our calves are leather, and sometimes they break.

The professional peloton is a place of applied

suffering. Though a bicycle race is a communal endeavour, you don't only race against other riders, though you do do this, but against yourself and the terrain you ride over. 'During the big races,' writes James Waddington in *Bad to the Bone*, a novel about murder in the peloton:

the competitors are reduced to fleshbags of blood and sinew. The usual appetites are suppressed. Everyone just works, eats and sleeps. Francesco Moser, weeks before he broke the hour record they sucked blood from his veins, separated out the red blood cells and froze them in glycerol, then at the last moment melted them and squirted them back into the living bloodstream. Legitimate, maybe, but it's close to vampirism for an honourable profession.

As spectators we consume the riders. Following the Tour, being a cycling fan, is a more intrusive form of fandom than that of most other sports. Racers submit to the gaze of the team manager, the coach, the *directeur sportif*. They do what they are told both on and off the bike. Cycling fans are themselves vampiric, suckling on the smallest titbits of information, condemning their heroes for doping on the smallest pieces of evidence. Cycling geeks read about the training regimes of their heroes, following weight fluctuations with all the dedication of *Daily Mail* journalists. Output and performance are measured in mechanical terms: in wattage and time.

There is a typology of cyclists' bodies which as a cycling fan you learn to interpret. The best climbers are birdlike creatures: hollow-boned and covered with a taught carapace of nerve and gristle, no extraneous bulk to speak of, which is all so much extra baggage. Sprinters are solid lumps of twitch muscle. Not over-bulked, not too lean, the time-trial specialist is a monotony artist. The best all round racers have the hypnotic ability to get into a rhythm and grind on and on, over any surface, for any amount of time.

The legibility of cyclists' bodies is apparent both to fans and to other riders. Gino Bartali – Italy's most famous pre-Second World War racing cyclist – used to instruct one of his team mates to watch the legs of his arch-rival, Fausto Coppi, and shout 'the vein' whenever an artery on Coppi's leg bulged, indicating that he was under duress. Then he would attack. Those massive varicosed legs, the products of years of doping, made Coppi's body as legible as a road-map, with its purple and green ribbons and its dendritic culs-de-sac.

You don't have to be an athlete to be a bicycle courier, but a few messengers have gone on to become professional racing cyclists. Graeme Obree – 'the Flying Scotsman' – worked as a courier in Edinburgh for a few years before he broke the hour record for cycling the furthest distance around a track in one hour on a bike he'd made himself from washing machine parts. Then there's the story of Nelson Vails, a New York messenger who went on to win a silver medal at the 1984 Olympic games before travelling to Japan to become a professional Kierin racer in the velodromes there. With stories like these there is just enough of a precedent to make us dream that we, too, might one day break away and join the peloton.

Evening was falling, and sun shone through the streets of Soho. People were leaving their offices. Packs of suited workers flowed through the square, en route to hitting the bars. Bears embraced on Great Compton Street. Girls tottered down the street, arm in arm. White van men tooted their horns at all comers, Friday night lairy.

Meanwhile, couriers were flocking to Soho Square like starlings coming in to roost. A murmuration of cyclists circled the square a few times before coming to rest, doing self-conscious laps, weaving between the walkers before leaning forward over their handlebars and skidding to a stop in long, drawn-out swerves, writing black rubber marks onto the tarmac. Others headed straight for the grass, dismounting their machines – leg over the handlebars in extended goose-steps – as they arrived by the gate, ghost-riding their bikes to a stop.

Most were there to drink, to wind down at the end of a week's work. They skinned up spliffs in their cupped hands as though reading their own palms. Tattooed elbows rose and fell, wavelike, drinking in

74

unison. They spat phlegm from beneath their spumy beards. Dreadlocks flailed in the evening breeze. Flashing chrome, pierced ears. Bike-punk cyber men and women loafed on the grass in lively indifference.

There was a buzz in the air. People were excited. Tonight's alleycat had been organised to raise money for a Dutch ex-messenger who had been diagnosed with cancer and wanted to visit his friends in Mexico one last time before he died. Simultaneous races were happening in cities across the world. It was the first race of the new season, and plenty of riders were itching to slough off the miseries of winter. They wanted to stretch their legs. All the old hands were there – Clarence, Darren, Mike, Simone. Over in the corner I spotted an obnoxious wild-man whose name I didn't know, who crashed parties and started fights, ruining things and boring you with his inane stories. His ever-present hat sat at an angle he thought of as rakish; his mouth with its tombstone teeth cracked into a permanent grin.

A group of younger riders were there too, most of whom I didn't recognise. There was a compact muscular man in a white cap riding a battered white bicycle with 'Anchor' written on the down-tube; a thin man with the bird-like body of a champion climber who was riding a geared time-trial bike; a thick-set sprinter on a pristine track bike. The man in the white cap said he had been a courier for a while a few years ago, but had grown bored of the work and had left. He wanted to join the army, he said, but he still came out to race every now and then. Alleycats are difficult things to give up.

As the sun set those who were planning to race eyed each other up surreptitiously. 'How are the legs?' we asked each other. 'I must have done about eighty miles today, so we'll see.' We hedged our bets. We talked ourselves down. No one wanted to come across as cocky. No one wanted to leave themselves open for an attack.

Beside me on the grass riders tinkered with their bicycles. A woman was fiddling with her wheels, tightening one spoke after another as though tuning a harp, until they pulled against each other in perfect, equal, tension. Someone else was fixing a puncture. I watched him expertly strip the tyre off, as though he was gutting a fish, peeling it off from around the rim of the wheel with a bent spoon. Once it lay open in front of him he pumped up the inner tube slightly, passing it across his lips to feel for the hole from which the air was escaping. Having located it he rubbed some vulcanising solution onto the rubber and waited for it to take effect. He placed a patch over the hole and massaged it into place. Once it had set he reassembled the tyre before fitting his wheel back onto his bike. The whole operation took seven minutes. You can do it in three if you carry a spare tube.

People stood around, drinking and smoking and doing track stands and wheelies and skids on their bikes. Others did laps of the square. People checked their bikes like ostlers checking the teeth and hooves of horses. They consulted their maps. They spoke excitedly about the race. I ate a banana. I tightened my chain and examined the sprocket on my back wheel. I knew it was fine: I'd worked on it all week, but I did it anyway as something to do.

The race was due to start at eight, but one and a half hours later we were still waiting. 'It's better to start later,' said Clarence, 'when it's dark. Then we can really own the streets'. Clarence is one of those haunting presences in the city. No one knows where he lives. He drifts across town from sofa to sofa, living out of his bag, moving across town in a slower, more drawn-out version of his daily working migrations.

Eventually the checkpoint marshals moved off to take up their positions. No one, apart from the organisers and the marshals, knew what the route of the race would be. The race was a blank space on the map ready to be filled, a known unknown. In most alleycat races there's no set route. You're given the first checkpoint, and must find your way there as quickly as possible. Get to the first checkpoint and you're given the address of the next one. Get there and move on to the next.

Eventually the organiser, John, assembles the racers and gives us a quick briefing. It's dusk by now. He tells us the Tour de Soho will be a gruelling ride, but not a long race. 'It's going to be quick. There are prizes for first to third place. It's a point-to-point run, but you will need an *A–Z*. The first checkpoint is on the corner of Northdown Street and Pentonville Road, at the bottom of the hill. Go!'

A Le Mans start. A scrum of bicycles and people. We run over to the pile of bikes and try to untangle them as quickly as possible before leaving the square. Bemused Friday night drinkers stand by watching. There's no time to cheer. I nod to Clarence and we jump over the wall next to the lawn on which we've assembled, grab our bikes, and run to the gate.

We begin to ride and immediately the bunch is split. One group heads north, the wrong way around the one-way system of the square and against the flow of traffic on Beak Street. The other heads south. I realise that I've picked the less direct route, and hope the leaders will be slowed by having to go against the traffic on the way through Soho, and that we'll be able to catch them. My group continue south down Lower John Street, then turn left onto Beak.

Up Wardour Street, past the throbbing traffic which waits idling at the lights, past the men in suits and girls in dresses drinking in the street in the balmy evening air, past the taxis queuing to sweep round onto Oxford Street and on to collect their fares, past other cyclists, blissfully unaware of the race taking place in their midst.

There are five or six of us in this group – Sam, Mike, Clarence, and a couple of other riders whose names I don't know, faces in the crowd who I half-recognise from the road.

At the top of Oxford Street I tuck in behind Sam and push till my lungs burn and my legs are beginning to throb, spinning down the gutter and shouldering my way through the gaps between cars and drinkers. Unlike a real road race, alleycats are scrappy, individual affairs. There's no real peloton, no real attempt to shield each other from the wind or help each other out on the climbs. The bunch is instantly fragmented, driven apart by the accidents of traffic and the interruptions of the lights. But still we try to work as a team, calling to each other as we navigate the temporary course, urging each other on. We grin as we go. We whoop and cheer. It is deeply antisocial, this run through the crowded streets of the West End, but for the moment we don't care. We are conscious only of the wind cracking around our ears, the pain in our legs, the rhythms of pedal stroke and the twitches from the handlebars as our wheels skip across the potholes in the tarmac beneath us.

'The dynamics of the Tour knows only four movements,' wrote Roland Barthes in his essay on the dynamics of bicycle racing, 'The Tour de France as Epic', 'to lead, to follow, to escape, to collapse':

To lead is the most difficult action, but also the most useless; to lead is always to sacrifice oneself; it is pure heroism, destined to parade character much more than assure results. *To follow*, on the contrary, is always a little cowardly, a little treacherous [...] *To escape* is a poetic episode meant to illustrate voluntary solitude.

A bicycle race is a communal endeavour, and it is almost impossible to win one on your own. This means that the moves you can make within a race are often purely symbolic. You can only attack with the tacit support of the group; only win if you're allowed to by the rest of the bunch. Marked men can't often break free on their own. A move made without support is a futile form of expression, a mute articulation of some kind rather than a genuine attempt to win.

It is a sport that has always rewarded, indeed depended on, symbolism. The peloton has its heroes and villains. Moves are made and clawed back. *Domestiques*, riders whose only role is to support the leaders of their team, sacrifice themselves heroically for their stars or treacherously go for glory on their own. Riders break and keep the lead only to be drawn inevitably back in to the bunch. The mock-heroic tone of much cycling writing reflects the sport's origins as a fundamentally literary event. From its inception, the Tour in particular was conceived of as an epic, and written about in an appropriately high style.

The bicycle race was often interpreted as a stage

for political symbolism also. The Tour was created in the wake of the Dreyfus affair by a young journalist named Géo Lefèvre, whose editor Henri Desgrange had asked him to come up with a way of boosting his paper's ailing sales. Before the advent of radio and television the results of the race were consumed like war: in print over breakfast, as lists of losses and gains. The yellow jersey worn by the leader of the Tour is the same colour as the pages of *L'Auto*, the newspaper which first organised the race.

Quickly appropriating Lefèvre's idea for a race that would take its riders around the whole of France, Desgrange's aim was to create 'the most courageous champions since antiquity', and the heroic era of cycling involved some of the most gruelling routes the organisers could dream up.

No one really knew what was going on out on the road during those early races. Cheating was rife. Riders took trains and had friends pick them up in cars along the route. One rider was once was caught being towed along the road by a car on a length of wire, the other end attached to a cork clamped between his teeth. During the first incarnation of the race Lefèvre was described by his son standing at night 'on the edge of the road, a storm lantern in his hand, searching in the shadows for riders who surged out of the dark from time to time, yelled their name and disappeared into the distance.'

Early cycling journalists were notorious for inventing facts, changing the positions of riders and fabricating knowledge of entire stages. On an early Tour the journalist Orio Vergani invented accounts of entire stages of races he hadn't seen. Later he reported that he had written about the race 'in the only way I could, that is, with my imagination'. In the early years the stories told about the Tour was much more important than the reality. Perhaps they still are.

When we hit Oxford Street the pack swerves hard right, round the front of a bus. Its passengers stare through the glass at us as we pass. We're gone before they grimace. We slalom through the oncoming traffic, against its flow. At the edge of Soho the pack fragments further. Half of us go up Tottenham Court Road. Two riders I don't know – one on a geared road bike, the other riding a bright blue single-speed – head down New Oxford Street for Bloomsbury. I follow them. It's a mistake. I don't quite know where we're going, but take my turn at the front of the bunch in any case.

At the end of Gray's Inn Road we run the lights, turn hard right and pedal against the oncoming traffic round the corner, crossing the lanes to face up the hill to attack Pentonville Road. At the checkpoint we catch up with another group of riders who've taken the shorter, faster route. We jostle for position, reaching out to grab the slips of paper held out by the marshals. I'm given a scrap of paper with the next checkpoint written on it: Duncan Terrace N1.

It's a straight run up the Pentonville Road from here, the only col on the circuit, part of the great escarpment that marks the northern edge of the Thames Basin. Standing off the saddle I run the red and push on my pedals, leaning forward into the gradient as I do so. The frame of my bicycle flexes as I lean left and right with each pedal stroke. It gives off quiet clicks and groans.

I've caught my legs unawares and they're perfectly willing for these few short minutes to really work for me. My skin too isn't up to speed quite yet – I'm dry as a bone, but I've invested in the future of my sweat. It'll come out no matter what I do, so I'll make the most of this dry patch and just push on up the hill. The Angel is nearly in view as I begin to feel a slight lactic burn in the legs, but it's nothing to worry about at this stage. Up and down they go, dancing on the pedals. My lungs crack. I grin like a fool.

Near the top of the hill my legs begin to burn. Cramp hits. Cars blur by. Other riders pass me. I reach out and grab hold of a bus lurching up the hill and catch a few stragglers at its brim. At the junction with Upper Street we open up again, stitching a way through the two lines of traffic under a hail of horn-honks and shouted swears.

I've started feeling good on the bike now, my legs feel strong and the run up the hill has opened my lungs. The saliva in my mouth has thickened to a paste which I spit out in solid chunks like broken teeth.

A white van forms a perfect shield for my break-away. Comforting clichés of graffiti are written in the dust covering its back window. Old time-trial racers used to set their records behind motorbikes or trains, using these vehicles, as I do now, as buffers to create pockets of turbulence in which they'd sit in comfort and pump enormous gear ratios to impossibly high speeds.

The white van just catches the next set of lights and I dash with it across the junction as it shields me from the traffic emerging from the right. Behind us I make out the tell-tale engine noise of a cab, a Fairfield, an old LTI model, which burbles like a piece of agricultural machinery as it swings round the bend and comes up behind. As an urban cyclist you quickly learn to attend to the soundscape of the city, anticipating vehicles coming up behind or emerging from side streets. The daily bombardment of sonic activity has honed my hearing, and I can recognise most generic types of vehicle through their aural signatures: the chugging tickover of a double-decker bus or the throaty hum of an aggressively driven white van.

The cab squeezes me into the curb, but as the traffic slows I leave it behind, tracing a route through the now stationary traffic and getting to the front of the line just as the lights change again. Another small hill. Lights in sequence. Open tarmac.

If bicycle track-races are lyric poems, and the one-day classics achingly significant short stories, then the grand Tours are triple-decker Victorian novels: sprawling, unpredictable, and filled with slightly artificial plot twists. Unlike football or tennis, sports that take place on standardised fields of play, cycling takes place in the real world. Its verisimilitude is its virtue: it celebrates the actual.

Unlike Football's World Cup, the grand Tours take place every year, and visit roughly the same territory each time – the riders make *la grande boucle* around France or do their circuits of Italy and Spain. In his wonderful cultural history of the Tour de France, Christopher Thompson argues that the geographic repetitiveness of the race was borne of necessity and opportunity. In Britain, earlier to industrialise than France, football became the national game because the large crowds available in industrialised cities meant that mass-spectatorship was easy to organise. France, a bigger country with a sparser population, needed a sport that came to them.

The great road races become exercises in applied topography, incubating notions of nationhood by measuring out countries by the turn of wheel and crank. Early coverage of the Tour gave many French people their first look at a map of France, popularising the idea of the country as 'L'Hexagone'. 'It has been said the Frenchman is not much of a geographer,' wrote Roland Barthes in *What is Sport?*:

his geography is not that of books, it is that of the Tour; each year, by means of the Tour, he knows the length of his coasts and the height of his mountains. Each year he recomposes the material unity of his country, each year he tallies his frontiers and his products.

Over the years the great climbs – Ventoux, Alpe d'Huez – have become as famous as the riders who annually attack them. In cycling journalism they're written about as characters with personalities and histories of their own. They are duplicitous. They possess motives. As Barthes continued, through the Tour – or at least through writing about the Tour:

Elements and terrain are personified, for it is against them that man measures himself, and as in every epic it is important that the struggle should match equal measures: man is therefore naturalised, Nature humanised. The gradients are *wicked*, reduced to difficult or deadly percentages, and the stages – each of which has the unity of a chapter in a novel (we are given, in effect, an epic duration, and an additive sequence of absolute crises and not the dialectical progression of a single conflict, as in tragic duration) – the stages are above all physical characters, successive enemies, individualised by that combination of morphology and morality which defines an epic Nature.

Later, as broadcasting technology improved, TV crews followed the race in cars and motorbikes: the bad feed registered something of the terrain, a series of interference bars and static fuzzing whenever the

Ottavio Bottecchia, first Italian winner of the Tour de France in
1924, does battle with the mountain.

peloton hit a particularly treacherous stretch of road.
Watching footage from the early Tours you're struck
by the utter ungainliness of the riders once they've dis-
mounted, to drink a quick cup of water at a dusty roadside bar, or to eat a quick meal after the day's racing.

Unlike standardised sports, the records for which
can be measured incrementally, year on year, there is
no necessity for ever-increasing improvement among
road cyclists. The terrain is the challenge. Thus it
doesn't much matter that the current peloton is sig-
nificantly slower than it was in the '90s. Far from it.

It's often held up as evidence that doping has, if not been stamped out, then been considerably reduced. When Fausto Coppi won the Tour in 1952 he rode up mountains as though they were hills. Great riders have the ability to turn the landscape to their whims, to dance up impossible inclines as though they are mere blips, and thus appear to physically alter the landscape itself.

The Danish filmmaker Jorgen Leth's masterpiece, *A Sunday in Hell* – a meticulously filmed documentary of the 1976 Paris–Roubaix spring classic (and arguably the greatest sports film ever made) – was revolutionary because his cameras went everywhere: filming from within the bunch from the backs of motorbikes; using big sweeping overhead shots from helicopters and cranes of the landscape over which the cyclists rode. After the race Leth followed the riders into the shower room, too, filming Roger de Vlaeminck and Eddie Merckx as they washed the Flanders mud from their bodies while they gave interviews to the press.

Once the Tour was a solo affair, but nowadays the peloton is followed by a vast caravan of vehicles. Team support cars carry bidons of water and spare wheels for their riders, all the while wirelessly monitoring their vital statistics. TV vans and motorbikes zip around getting their shots, and the dreaded 'broom wagon' brings up the rear, sweeping up exhausted riders as it goes.

It's still difficult to know how best to watch the race. Fans who congregate along the route spend most of their time in dusty little bars, watching events unfold on television before rushing outside for a few minutes as the peloton whirrs by. Other, more devoted disciples seek the stigmata of their heroes, riding the route themselves during L'Ètape du Tour. Still, a visit from the peloton can do wonders for a village's tourist industry, and the waiting list to host a stage finish is years long.

Before each stage is ridden fans pore over the maps. We assess the climbs, identifying those points at which sprinters might attack, those moments at which the climbers might have their day. We assess road surfaces, more or less authoritatively. Then, when the race begins, we watch online, hogging the bandwidth, following the video streams and live blogs. We download the Tour apps and refresh them endlessly. Little avatars of the riders let us know who's in the lead. We log onto obscure websites where the power data collected from the riders by the team cars can be read in real time. We note their wattage output and the gear ratios they're riding. We imagine what it must be like to be them.

Time and distance have passed, registered only in the sweat that's now leaving its tide-marks on my jersey and its salt-crust on my brow. The hill's taken it out of me, and keeping enough energy in the tank to accelerate away from junctions is important in a race like this.

As I reach the next checkpoint I grab the next tag – The Highway, Barbican.

When I get to the Barbican I carry my bike up the stairs next to the station before getting lost in the Ballardian labyrinth of its walkways. I bunny-hop down small flights of stairs. People shout at me as I pass. Eventually, by following the flashing red lights of other racers, I find the next checkpoint and descend again to street level.

We're sent on to Holland Street, over the river in SE1. I'm flagging but the race still feels urgent. I approach via the humpbacked Southwark Bridge, but when I get to the south side I make a mistake and turn east rather than west. I get to Borough before I realise my mistake, get out my map, and head back towards Tate Modern, where a huddle of marshals are waiting for me. I've lost all the other riders I was racing with by now, but as I head back over the river I spot the man in the white cap. He's riding hard and fast, but has cut his leg in a fall, and blood flows from the wound as he rides along. When he sees me he accelerates and leaves me for dust, despite his injury. I'm chastened. I'm empty and have nothing to answer him with. After a minute or two all I can see is his rear light winking in the distance.

I'm on my own now, and just want the race to be over. I tack down Shaftesbury Avenue towards the next checkpoint on Burlington Gardens. I spot another group of riders heading back east, and follow them to

Warner Street EC1, tucked away under a bridge in the valley of the River Fleet. I know my race is over. There's only one checkpoint left, back where we started in W1. A group of us race back to Golden Square in a daze, riding three abreast down the middle of Theobald's Road. I don't talk to anyone. I can't, I've nothing left. But eventually we make it back to the finishing line.

I've not done well. Out of thirty-two racers I've come somewhere in the middle of the pack, I tell myself, but everyone's stopped counting by then. None but the top three places count. As I wait, chest heaving, legs twitching, a few other riders come in. One rides round the square before jumping off his bike and letting it roll on down the middle of the road. It nearly hits a pristine Mercedes parked by the kerb.

Prizes are awarded, but no one is paying much attention. Fastest to complete the course is a quiet Polish man with huge plugs in his ears. The prospective soldier riding the white Anchor frame, who left me for dust as we crossed the river, comes second. He's pleased. Third is a young Brazilian guy called Theo, taking part in his first race in London. He smiles. He is composed. I wheeze on the pavement as more riders come in. Someone passes me a bottle of cider.

Darren mocks my pathetic finish, my lack of racing nous, the weakness of my legs and of my geographic knowledge. John gets on someone's shoulders to thank us all for racing. We discuss the race. People do laps of the square. Others throw up discreetly into the gutter.

I spit thick flecks of phlegm from between my teeth. My lungs burn.

Later, we all depart for an after party in a squat on Whitfield Street, opposite a police station. A fight breaks out. Mike comes out with a fire extinguisher and douses the fighters, but they carry on regardless. I leave as more fights break out. The next day I wake up covered in bruises.

A few months after the race, I was leaning on a grit-bin outside the Natural History Museum. Winter had set in. The roads crunched with ice where they weren't slicked with oil. I was waiting to meet Paul Fournel, the author who most directly seemed to address the cyclogeographic ideas I'd been thinking about. I had discovered that he was working as the French Cultural Attaché in London. I wanted to talk to him about the idea of the bicycle race, so central to French cultural identity, so absent from our own. I couriered him a letter: could I meet him? He invited me round on his last day, his last hour, in London, to talk about cycling, literature, and the mythology of the bicycle race.

The lift was out of order at his office on Cromwell Road, so I walked up the stairs. 'So you're a cyclist who can climb stairs as well?' he asked as I got to the top. His office was spartan, apart from a bookshelf, desk and computer. Biographies of cyclists lined the shelves. Fournel was packing up to leave for France. I told him I

wanted to meet a real writer. He asked me about couriering. 'Do you work for yourself?' We talked about the
logistics of the job, about the employment regulations
and labour and about knowing London. He asked me
what gear ratio I favoured. Cycling stories are like fishing stories. They are told not to inform the listener but,
as in the confessional, to unburden the teller.

I asked Fournel what he thought of London
cycling culture. Did he ride here? Had he found a
peloton to join? He rode laps round Richmond Park,
he said. He'd just got back from a holiday in France.
Wistfully he described the hills he'd conquered on
that last trip.

We talked about Boris bikes and the Parisian
equivalent, the Velibs, the people's bikes. 'There are
problems,' he said, 'it's amazing how people vandalise
or steal these bikes – they throw them into the Seine.
They hang them in trees. I've even heard of one that
appeared in Australia. Imagine the effort involved in
that, the cost of shipping it over and so on? It's very
strange. So now I make sure I check the bikes very
carefully before I take them out of the cradle. I check
the tyres are pumped, that the gears and brakes work
and so on.'

I asked him about his own bikes. He'd recently
bought a Condor bicycle with a titanium frame, which
he loved because he was getting old and it ran a tiny
gear, good for attacking the hills: 'It's a beautiful bike,
and cheap compared to most others. I don't like carbon

fibre, it is too unforgiving, it feels like you are riding an arrow, you know?'

He asked me if I rode a single speed. He told me that not many people ride fixed-gear in Paris, because of the hills. 'But they do in San Francisco,' I said. 'Yes, but in San Francisco they don't ride up the hills. I lived there for a while. What they do is grab on to cars or trams and get pulled up the hills, then just coast down. They probably cycle less than couriers in any other country. But it is very dangerous, incredibly dangerous.'

I asked him about his writing, about the connections between cycling, bicycle racing and literature. Why did he think the bike lent itself to this kind of literary treatment?

'Not just literature but all media,' he said. 'The newspaper of course, which in fact sponsored the early Tours de France, and largely invented bicycle racing, and then the radio and now the TV. The bicycle is a literary vehicle, a good place to think. But also, in bicycle racing at any rate, the day-by-day narrative of a race is very good for a reader, is very easy to digest. I think these are themes and ideas that are always attractive.' We discussed the Dutch author Tim Krabbé's novel *The Rider*, the finest evocation of a bicycle race ever written. In it Krabbé describes an amateur one-day classic from the perspective of one of the racers. The race is described kilometre by kilometre, every inch ridden corresponding to a narrative twist or turn. It's a book about the essential drama of the road, and the stories that unfold around the personalities of a race.

Fournel's book, like Krabbé's, is part of a canon of cycling literature that is more thoughtful than auto-biographies of cyclists and books about the history of the bicycle race. There is a great literary tradition, es-pecially in France, Holland and Ireland, of combining philosophical speculation with descriptions of cycling, and I wanted to know why he had found the bicycle to be such a potent vehicle for philosophical specula-tion.

'I think because it's so simple, but it remains a mystery,' he said. 'You know I ride in a bunch in Paris, a group of friends. And one of them is a physicist at the Sorbonne, one of the twelve top physicists in the world or something. And even he cannot explain it, cannot tell me how a bike and rider stay upright. It has some-thing to do with the wobble of the front wheel, the way it moves from side to side, but really we don't know. I think this is one reason it is so attractive to writers: it is an enigma that can be pondered forever. But teaching people to ride is also an amazing thing, something they will never forget. I've taught many people to ride, or to love to ride: girlfriends, friends, children, and I always love the fact that they will remember that forever, both the event and the action which is taught.'

Fournel needed to finish packing, so I got up to leave. We shook hands. 'Come visit me in Paris,' he said. 'I'd love to,' I replied. I think I will. 'We can ride the Velibs together, I'll show you the city,' he said as he led me to the stairs. In my copy of *Need for the Bike* he had written: 'For Jon, "Le cycliste des rues de Londres", these memories of the countryside.'

A year or so after my encounter with Fournel, I went to compete in the international Cycle Messenger World Championships, the closest thing on the courier calendar to one of the great Tours. The championships, the CMWCs, are an odd mix of trade-show, music festival and gymkhana, and are unlike any other bicycle race in the world.

The main race is designed to mimic a working day, but unlike an alleycat race it is run on a closed course. Checkpoints represent the offices to which messengers would normally deliver, and empty packages are exchanged for signatures while the clock keeps score. Competitors start the race with a manifest, a list of jobs and delivery addresses, and must work their way around the checkpoints as efficiently and quickly as possible. Fake thieves lie in wait, ready to steal the bikes of racers who neglect to lock them up. At some checkpoints you'd be searched and your stash confiscated. At others you'd be made to wait around until your package was ready. At some you had to jump through bicycle tyres or do a shot of vodka before the marshals would sign your manifest.

The CMWCs are usually quite an unsophisticated

affair. In 2010 the race took place in Panajachel, a tiny town in the Guatemalan highlands, and resembled something from *Mad Max*. Guatemalans are allowed to carry guns, as long as they're kept on display, and a few messengers in Panajachel sported pistols alongside the radios and mobile phones which they carry strapped across their chests. Some of the events were nearly cancelled when 'La Ocho', the figure-of-eight shaped track that was due to host some of the races, was swept away in floods, along with several homes. It was rebuilt overnight. When the finals of the track races eventually took place they were illuminated by car headlights.

The year I went the competition was being held in Poland. 'Warsaw has had it pretty rough over the last century,' I read in the welcome pack for the competition. 'First the Germans had a dream to turn her into a lake, then the Russians rebuilt her using cheap ass Russian concrete slabs, making her grey and dull.' Most of the city, I learnt, was destroyed during the Second World War, after which much of the old town was laboriously reconstructed brick-by-brick.

The race was to take place on a peninsula jutting out into the River Vistula from the west bank of the city, near to where, at the end of the war, the Polish Home Army had waited for Soviet support that never came. A grand brutalist sculpture of a minesweeper commemorates the failed uprising. At racer registration I was given a number and a map of the peninsula.

The course was roughly the size of a small city block, criss-crossed by tracks and punctuated by twenty-six checkpoints. Streets were named things like 'Skid Row,' and 'Main Stage Alley.'

Modern Warsaw is not particularly bicycle-friendly. Vast, multi-lane roads cleave the city into fragments, while a complicated system of flyovers and bridges take you on mad and terrifying detours. We were warned to beware of the police, who come down hard on drunk cycling. As I cycled back to my hostel on a rented bike I noticed little covens of messengers dotted around the city, cruising the streets in packs or huddling together looking at maps. On a cycle path next to the Royal Lazienki park I got talking to a man from Vienna whose bicycle had been stolen from out-side a club the night before, and who was trying to find a replacement. 'I still need to work when I get back,' he murmured sadly, as he clattered off down the street, walking awkwardly in his stiff-soled cycling shoes.

A pair of cyclists pulled up next to me. They told me that a courier from Dublin had been hit by a car the previous night while crossing the Solec, an enormous multi-lane motorway that runs by the river alongside the race course. He'd been hit hard, his bike had been destroyed and he was in a coma in hospital.

Later that evening, under a concrete flyover, the messenger tribes of the world gathered. I bumped into friends from London who'd driven to Warsaw in one mad dash, relying on amphetamines and coffee to keep awake. Within hours of arriving their driver had been arrested for cycling with a can of beer in his bidon holder, and the others were trying to get him bailed. They were worried that he'd been caught with pockets full of drugs, enough to land him a lengthy prison sentence in Poland. As we were just about to cycle to the police station to see if they'd let him go, he rolled up sheepishly on his bike. 'They never checked my pockets,' he said, 'just put me in the back of the van. So I ate all the speed.' He already had glassy eyes and a wild stare. He would stay awake for the rest of the week, growing increasingly confused and belligerent.

Mosquitoes swarmed in the dampness of the forest. The rain fell. No one wanted to talk about the messenger from Dublin.

On the second day we assembled under the Łazienkowski Bridge on the peninsula to watch the qualifications. A steady stream of competitors walked through race HQ, collected their manifests and set off to navigate their way round the course. Race officials tramped around making sure they obeyed the rules of the road, admonishing those who ignored the one-way systems and confiscating the bikes of riders who neglected to lock them up. Some messengers competed on foot, and did well. Others cheated, discovering unmarked tracks and secret routes through the forest. A pair of messengers raced on a tandem. I sat at a checkpoint in the forest for a while. Occasionally messengers would emerge from the trees, ask if they were in the right place, and cycle off again.

The organiser of the race, a messenger from Amsterdam named Fish, explained to me how he had designed the race using a complicated logistical algorithm that could be applied to any course. He said that his system would revolutionise the world of competitive alleycat racing, standardising its rules and allowing objective trans-competition comparisons to be made. I cycled to another checkpoint and watched the stream of competitors slip down a muddy hill. The course was strangely quiet, far removed from the usual sounds of a working day.

In the afternoon the sun came out, and a large crowd gathered round an old car, which had been wheeled out for the wing mirror smashing competition. Competitors had to cycle alongside the car and knock off a mirror stuck on with Velcro, with points awarded for distance and style. Some tried to kick with one foot while pedalling with the other, but the most effective strategy was to use a D-lock as a bat. Eventually people got bored of the controlled destruction and the competition degenerated into a near-riot. The car was kicked to pieces and smashed up with locks before being overturned and almost ending up in the river. Someone tried to set it on fire before one of the organisers climbed on top and asked people to stop as the car was to be used as the winner's podium. Across the water, a pair of old men who'd been quietly fishing withdrew, and eventually the police turned up.

That evening I sat by a fire tended by a dread-locked, moonfaced man from Budapest, who admonished people for upsetting his shopping-trolley grill. A friendly drunkard stumbled over and sat down heavily on the embers. The comforting stench of several hundred messengers drifted up on the evening air. Bored by the rain, I left the campsite a few hours later and drifted back into the city, guided by a Polish messenger who I knew from London. Halfway home he showed me a street of clubs and bars, on one side of which stood an empty, half-finished office building, dotted with clubbers taking the air. Couples sat with their legs dangling from its empty windows like figures in a doll's house. We locked our bikes, climbed through a fence and explored the concrete skeleton of the building, before sitting down on the roof and watching the lights of the city.

On the third day, my last in Warsaw, I wandered round the racecourse on foot. No working London messengers had qualified for the main race. In the hours before it began, the most serious competitors sat studying maps of the course which they'd drawn on their arms in permanent marker. Some tinkered with their bikes, adjusting gears and brakes that had become clogged with mud. Riders who hadn't qualified for the finals, or couldn't be bothered to race, relaxed in a homemade jacuzzi which the team from Lausanne had brought with them. Steam rose into air, meeting the rain half way.

During the final race I helped man a checkpoint in the winds and rain whilst bedraggled cyclists emerged from the mists and presented their soggy manifests to be stamped. Our umbrella was blown away in a gust and drifted dangerously towards the Vistula. Along the Solec, the road next to us that runs along the river, a professional peloton roared by. The Tour of Poland had come to town, conducting a five-lap circuit of Warsaw. We cheered them on: *allez! allez!* One rider had his dick in his hand and let fly a steady stream of piss as he rolled along, pushed on by his teammate. The messenger from Dublin was still in hospital. I heard no more about him.

5

– Off the Map –

Not to find one's way in a city may well be uninteresting
and banal. It requires ignorance – nothing more. But to lose
oneself in a city – as one loses oneself in a forest – that calls
for a quite different schooling. Then, signboard and street
names, passers-by, roofs, kiosks, or bars must speak to the
wanderer like a cracking twig under his feet in the forest.
        – Walter Benjamin, *A Berlin Chronicle*

For the psychogeographers the map, and knowing
where you were on it, constituted a threat. Maps
divorce people from the world they inhabit, encour-
aging them to believe that they live in a virtual, un-
touchable environment, and reducing the landscape to
a series of easily navigable coordinates. It is a fear that
has only become more general with the rise of satnav
and the smartphone. Maps like these record official
versions of the world, telling us where to go and how
to get there, and in doing so they maintain control. For
the psychogeographers, going off the map was seen as
a way of reclaiming the world.

As a courier I'd found that cycling was a good way
of resisting the tyranny of maps. Bikes, like water, want
to flow downhill and cycling tends to uncover, almost

unconsciously, the old waterways and trade routes of a landscape. Ride a bike in London and you often find yourself following the ancient ley-lines of the city's subterranean rivers. The pull feels curiously elemental – your bicycle becomes a dowsing rod. I discovered many of London's lost rivers in this way – the Fleet, flowing from the ponds of Hampstead Heath to the river Thames, through Kentish Town and Camden, through Bloomsbury and Clerkenwell under Farringdon Road; the Walbrook, bisecting the City from Shoreditch to Bank; the Tyburn, which starts in Regent's Park and trickles on through the West End, crossing Oxford Street just north of Grosvenor Square. The rivers had worn away the fabric of the city, and the bicycle made the dips and rises they left behind legible.

Along with the rivers I'd sketched out the city's geological features. Day after day I circled the lip of the basin of the River Fleet. Day after day I climbed and descended the Pentonville escarpment. I skimmed alongside the reclaimed foreshore of the River Thames, the flattest route between City and the West End. Later I'd confirm the existence of London's geological contours on maps, but their discovery was made by bicycle. I felt like I was engaged in a process of what the writer and suburban explorer Nick Papadimitriou calls 'deep topography', using the bicycle as a way of communing with the landscape's ancient, and unmapped, past.

Open a topographical map of London, like R. W. Mylne's *London and its Environs, Topographical and*

Geological, and you'll see how the London basin has been formed by these secret waterways over the years. Mylne's map is a beautiful document, an abstract mass of gradated colours and lines which follow the contours of the city itself. Pink and green streaks highlight the city's Bagshot sands, its siliceous mounds, its loamy clays and its pebble beds. This map was for me a document of confirmation - its hachures and spot-heights corresponded to the gradients I had felt during the day's circuits, confirming the testimony of my legs.

Mylne's map was a by-product of the massive expansion of Victorian London that had fuelled the period's craze for geological and archaeological exploration. Mapping London in this way was as much diagnostic as it was descriptive. 'As much as Bazalgette and Chadwick,' writes Eric Robinson, 'Mylne must be associated with the major improvements to the public health of the overgrown Victorian city and conurbation in the latter part of the nineteenth century.' Mapping the city was a way of improving London, exposing its dark secrets – its pockets of illness and poverty – and bringing them to consciousness. As tunnels were dug to house the new sewerage network, and to serve the underground trains that were burrowing themselves through the loam, so London's geology came to the surface to be scrutinised.

Before the nineteenth century the study of London's geology had been a speculative affair, the product of occasional boreholes dug into the surface of the city but never consummated into a general, mappable, trend. The cuttings for the new subsurface railways and especially the road improvement works in the late nineteenth century mapped London's past as well as its present. In Archway fossils were unearthed: plates of turtle shell and crocodile scale, seeds of the Nipa palm, sharks teeth buried in the London clay, all testifying to the city's equatorial prehistory. Up over London, at the top of Highgate Hill, amber was uncovered. As Robinson records, 'masses of coagulated resin of tropical trees, sometimes containing the remains of flies and insects of the same moist forests' inspired sublime thoughts of geological deep time. In 1836, the London Clay Club was formed, and Karl Marx was 'introduced to the wonders of the Archway Cutting' and the inevitability of historical materialism by his friend, the geologist Roche Dakyns.

Iain Sinclair is an underground avatar for a particular kind of urban writing, a deep topography all of his own. He has been investigating London's past and present (its overground and underground spaces) by foot from his Hackney-based home for decades, stitching narratives together as he moves around the city. The method is familiar by now. Journeys are made through landscapes and archives, conversations transcribed into notebooks and sutured into taut, endlessly fertile prose. He writes in the tradition of the visionary walker-poet

– William Blake, John Clare, W. G. Sebald – but he is interested mainly in stories about the overlooked and the forgotten. 'I've always been fascinated by pests like Thomas De Quincey,' he wrote in *American Smoke*, a book documenting a journey through America, which was also a quest for his own stylistic origins, 'the way he hiked to the Lake District and attached himself to Wordsworth and Coleridge, before "betraying" them with gossip and mangled histories.'

Sinclair doesn't like the term psychogeography any more but he can't get away from it. His prose is hammered out in shoe leather. Partly it's the kind of urban access you get on foot that he finds attractive. In *London Orbital* he described a year-long walk around the 'acoustic footprint' of the M25. In *Edge of The Orison* he retraced the poet John Clare's mad walk in search of his dead wife from his asylum in Epping Forest and out through Essex. My London, which I'd grown up in and discovered through cycling, was also largely formed from reading his books.

I wanted to talk to him about cycling, the literature of mapping, and the city he has spent so long walking in, and so I couriered a letter to Sinclair, having gleaned his address from one of his old book dealing catalogues. One of the advantages of being a courier is that the garb – grubby bag and official-looking radio – grants anonymity and access, and I presented myself as being on official business. Or perhaps it's because he's used to uninvited visitors. Over the years Sinclair has become the centre of a circuit that encompasses all of London. Writers plan trudges across the city with his house in mind as their destination. Strangers turn up on his doorstep seeking blessings, offering files of secret photographs, little magazines, scraps of map with their mad schemes drawn on them. They seek benediction and, like a friendly parish priest, Sinclair gives them time. He tells them what they want to hear.

He is no longer much of a cycling fan, but in *Hackney, that Rose-Red Empire*, a 'confidential report' of the borough he has lived in for decades, he describes exploring Hackney by bike. The 'sharp-saddled bicycle was a collaborator in any reading of the city,' he writes, 'territory crossed and crisscrossed: burial grounds and back rivers explored.'

I had brought a copy of a book with me, a wartime edition of Flann O'Brien's 'Cruiskeen Lawn' column for the *Irish Times,* which O'Brien had written under the nom de plume – one of many – 'Myles na gCopaleen'. It was a samizdat edition printed on thick, war-rationed paper. I knew Sinclair was a fan, and O'Brien's abiding interest in the metaphysical secrets of the bicycle seemed like an appropriate context within which to approach the question of a putative cyclogeography with Sinclair. A few weeks before we met I'd gone to a screening of Chris Petit's film *The Cardinal and the Corpse*, a film about book dealing in the East End for which Sinclair had been hired as 'freak wrangler'. The cast were a catalogue of shady types, the people I'd read about for years in Sinclair's books: Drifield the book dealer, bristling with slick dodginess; sci-fi visionary Michael Moorcock; the magician and comic book writer Alan Moore. The title of the film was significant too. It was taken from a book in the *Sexton Blake* series of boys-own adventure stories, rumoured to have been written by O'Brien under the name 'Stephen Blakesley'.

When I arrived, Sinclair asked me to help him take in his recycling, grabbing a bin and pointing to a brown bag. In his Hackney book he writes of the perniciousness of our burgeoning eco-consciousness, the sinister way in which both cycling and recycling are becoming articles of faith rather than innocent activities. Soon there will be 'knife fights in the street over blue bins with the wrong category of potato peel,' he writes. We wheeled the bin through his house – neat, stuffed with books, orderly. 'Where's your bike?' he asked, 'Do you want to bring it in? Have you locked it up? Bikes are currency now, round here.' I told him it would be fine: though a thoroughbred, it is camouflaged by its shabbiness.

Sinclair is tall and looks younger than his seventy years. It must be all that walking. His sitting room was full of pictures of birds. Beat-poetry books lined the shelves. A photograph of him riding a swan-shaped pedalo down the Regent's canal looked down from the mantelpiece. It was a souvenir from *Swandown*, a film he made with Andrew Kötting for which they rode a pedalo from Hastings to London on England's secret waterways, a different kind of cyclogeographic *dérive*.

One thing that I'd always found attractive about Sinclair's writing is the way it seems to map places I knew so well, but does so askew, as in a fairground mirror, uncovering overlooked perspectives and realities along the way. His work is both deeply local and strangely prophetic: it makes connections, makes public the secret networks of the city that would otherwise feel exclusive, and in conversation he's the same. In between sentences he pulls books off his shelves and passes them to me, marshalling his evidence. Sinclair is used to this, to talking. Start him off and he gains momentum. Like a bicycle, in motion he gains stability. He knows what you're there for – information loads, contact with some just-lost past.

Though he was welcoming he was wary of bikes, and somewhat hostile towards them. 'Cycling is filling up the gaps,' he told me. 'After the canal path, it's the pavements. We're evolving into centaurs on wheels.' It's partly the misplaced nostalgia of the new cycling lobby he objects to, he said – the way the bicycle has ceased to be a subversive machine, as it was in the work of O'Brien and Beckett, but is now associated with nostalgic projections of an England that never was. In an essay for the *London Review of Books* a few years ago he described the new demographics that have emerged around the MAMIL – the 'middle-aged man in lycra' – and the cult of the bike which attends him. He described 'the Lycra-clad, peloton-inhabiting, short-haul commuter. They charge to work, Haggerston to Hoxton, Camden to Canary Wharf, as a yellow-tabarded bicycle race, dedicated to the legend of Alfred Jarry.' By the year 2000, Sinclair wrote, the 'modest and marginal eccentricity' of the bicycle had been almost completely swept aside in favour of something far more sinister.

I asked Sinclair about his views on London cycling nowadays. 'My relation to cycling is very complex,' he said. 'There was a time when cycling represented a sort of freedom, it gave you the freedom to cycle somewhere: across to Hackney Marshes, or down to Limehouse or wherever, to do the job and come back. The only people cycling were at working level in the city. When I was a gardener all the gardeners arrived by bicycle, because they wouldn't have been able to afford cars. On the Lea, on the towpath, the only bicycles would be ridden by fishermen going off to the country, or occasionally those sort of English eccentrics – cyclists in the old style, train-spotter types. It was very hard to cycle then because they had barriers in front of every single bridge. It was a bit of a battle to go out, and you had to be careful to give precedence to walkers and people with kids, which now is just not the case at all. Quite the reverse.'

He'd written his novel *Radon Daughters* from the saddle, using the bike to get out to the limits of London in a few hours, giving himself time to return home and write in the afternoon while things were still fresh in his mind. But these days he is 'deeply suspicious' of the bicycle, suspicious of its appropriation by politicians and bankers, not as a tool for work but as a means of colonising the city. 'It is a perpetual battle,' he said. 'There are a few times I've been driving through London in the early evening and been surrounded by packs of sort of aggrieved respect-demanding cyclists, on all sides. It's like driving through wolves. There is this sense of correctness: of "look what I've achieved." All that makes me really stand back from it. You take your life in your hands when you cross these cycle paths.'

It is easy to share Sinclair's hesitancy over the fanatical single-mindedness of the contemporary cycling lobby, but as a courier I'd found that the bike can still provide an escape, a way of hiding in plain sight. During the London riots in 2011 I'd cycled down to Clapton, hooded up, weaving through the throng and watching its exuberant destructiveness from the saddle. It was a perfect way of bearing witness. As long as your bike wasn't too expensive-looking, and you didn't have a shiny camera dangling round your neck, you were left alone. The bike provided a semblance of mob mentality and the ability to get away quickly if need be.

Nevertheless the utopian schemes of the modernist cyclists seemed pretty far away from the world Sinclair described, and I wanted to know what he thought of the future of cycling. Could it be reclaimed as a subversive activity, despite the branding, despite the hugely inflated bicycling costs, despite the surveillance of Boris bike tracking and the potential for political appropriation? Was David Cameron's much-publicised cycling commute to the Commons (during which he was followed by a chauffeur-driven car containing a change of clothes and his security detail) the death-knell for any kind of cycling utopianism? Was there any hope for a resurgent cyclogeographic tradition as radical as Jarry's? 'I'm not encouraged to get back on a bike,' he said. 'I might do from time to time. I might do in another place. The south coast. You can get that much further much more easily. But I hate the idea of having to lock it up, carrying this great thing because otherwise it's gone. I used to cycle to Victoria Park, leave the bike in the bushes, run round the park and cycle home. Now, I think you wouldn't be able to take your eyes off it, unless you've got a complete wreck. Even the wrecks are desirable now. There's a shop – I don't know if it's still there – that used to specialise in that sort of retro look. Tweedy jackets and wicker baskets. It's bizarre.'

Sinclair was winding down. He'd said his piece. He was interested in bicycle couriering, in the endgame of the career. 'What's an old courier supposed to do?' he asked me. They become controllers, I said, or cabbies. Or they die on the road. Forty seems to be the point at which the body wants to give up. 'That's the nice thing about walking, you can go on a bit longer', he said.

Inspired by my encounter with Sinclair, I wanted to get out of London, to the edge of things. He had tipped me off about Nigel Henderson, an artist and photographer who had lived in Bethnal Green after the war and made a series of what he called 'stressed photographs' of boys riding their bikes around the East End in the 50s and 60s.

Henderson was interested in the way his photographic images captured something of the movement of the cyclists themselves, the way in which an apparently objective record of an action could be manipulated to suggest the action described. It was a curious form of subjective indexicality. 'I noticed,' Henderson explained:

> that when I had an actual negative that interested me (let's say a boy on a bicycle) I could sometimes enrich the impact of the image by slanting the paper under the enlarger projecting lens [...] If I pleated the paper horizontally I could create a pattern of stress which further animated the situation by putting the wheels and frame 'through it' as it were and creating an identification with the boys' efforts and the tension of the wheels and frame in a somewhat 'Futurist' way.

I was fascinated by Henderson's stressed photographs of cyclists, and Sinclair had told me about another potential cyclogeographic *dérive*, one that seemed

Nigel Henderson's stressed photograph of a cyclist

to fulfil the themes of cycling as a kind of topograph-ical mapping. It was to follow Henderson on a ride down the Northern Sewage Outfall, part of the great anti-cholera sewer system built by Joseph Bazelgette in the 1860s, which runs from Wick Lane in Hackney to Beckton in east London. Sinclair had told me that Henderson used regularly to stalk the great pipe, walk-ing and cycling along its length, exploring the territory as he went. No one was on a bicycle then at all, he had said, just Henderson and the odd fisherman.

One spring day I tried to follow the line described by the outfall – now sanitised and branded as a cycle friendly 'greenway' – from the River Lea, near to where I lived, to Beckton. It wasn't a satisfactory journey. After I'd wrangled with the guts of the Olympic site, where bored security guards manned every junction, turning me back, and where the razor-wired watch-towers made the landscape look like something from a Second World War movie, I found the greenway. The ride along the length of the pipe was uneventful, save for the occasional whiffs of piss and shit you got along the way, drifting from the pipe. The landscape was sparse, post-industrial.

When I got to Beckton I climbed the Beckton Alps, imagining myself climbing one of the great cols – Alpe d'Huez, perhaps, or Mont Ventoux, where the British cyclist Tommy Simpson died in the heat, far above the tree line, during the 1967 Tour de France, his body broken by fatigue and jumped up on amphetamines and brandy. In the distance stood the old gas works, used as a stand-in for the Vietnamese city of Huế dur-ing the filming of Stanley Kubrick's *Full Metal Jacket*. The place still had an air of scorched earth about it. Burnt-out park benches lined the route, and many of the tracks were fenced off. Ten thousand people used to work here, manning the gas works, but now it lies largely empty. I climbed the weaving path that winds up the hill to its highest point and clambered through a gap in the fence, where a couple were kissing in the shadow of a fence across which several large crosses of St George had been painted. They didn't welcome the intrusion, and so I slipped away, back along the pipe, back into the city.

Couriering is constrained navigation. You're constrained by the demands of commerce – by the companies that book the work, by the layout of the industrial sectors of the city (PR, design and fashion in the east, media and commerce in the middle, publishing and boutique retail in the west) – but also by the shapes and contours of the roads themselves. Maps are historical records of these constraints, which change over time. In the city especially the memories contained in maps are only tentative. Roads become blocked and one-way systems are enforced, seemingly overnight, in order to accommodate the long-term projects that keep the city moving. For the past few years Crossrail has been redrawing the London map around itself, and a huge development in Victoria has channelled cyclists and drivers through vast metal channels in a temporary re-mapping of the area, killing cyclists implacably as it goes.

The London map, as experienced by its cyclists, is created around these temporary hot spots and re-workings, and thus is inherently fluid. There is no such thing as an accurate map of London: there are instead only records of what it was, or imagined projections of what it might become. Many maps of London include streets that have never existed, even in the eyes of the planners. 'Trap Streets' they're called, and they're used to catch out would-be copyright infringers, built-in errors used to assert their maker's intellectual property.

For couriers maps are essential tools of the trade, but they are always provisional and partial. Most couriers use the *A–Z*, but more and more riders these days use their smartphones to navigate. The maps used by some of the older riders are personal documents that they've amended with scribbled hieroglyphs: notes on buildings that only let you in through the back entrance or only at certain times of day; footnotes recording the rhythms and reliability of particular goods lifts; Post-its warning of the presence of aggressive postroom workers at various locations across the city.

London's most famous cartographer is, or at any rate should be, Phyllis Pearsall, the creator of the *A–Z*. The story of Pearsall's map – conceived by the young artist in 1935 as she wandered Belgravia looking for a party armed only with an inadequate Ordinance Survey map of the area – is told as an epic, but it's really a love story. And, like all love stories, there is a strong element of mythology to it. Struck by the insufficiency of the existing maps of London, it is said that Pearsall spent a year walking every one of London's twenty thousand streets for ten hours a day. By night she drew her map.

One of her great innovations was to obtain a list of street-name changes from the London County Council in order to update her new map of London (a box of 'T's blew out of the window of her office onto High Holborn, she later recalled, and so in the first *A–Z* Trafalgar Square didn't have an entry in the index). Eventually she conquered London's 3,000 miles of streets and inscribed them all onto paper. Roads took precedence, in scale, over buildings and green spaces. If Harry Beck's tube map was a work of abstraction, Pearsall's map was an impressionist masterpiece. It was a difficult book to sell at first, but eventually W. H. Smith agreed to stock her map, the first edition of which Pearsall delivered to shops herself in a wheelbarrow. The *A–Z* was a map which had governed my daily experience of the city for years, but now I wanted to leave it behind, to find out what lay beyond it.

Almost fifty years ago, while he was still a student at Central St Martin's School of Art, the artist Richard Long embarked on a different kind of mapping: a bicycle ride from WC1 to Cambridgeshire. A photo of him about to set off shows a young, steely-eyed man carrying a rucksack and standing beside his road bike, a simple six-speed machine with mud guards and dropped handlebars. To the top tube of his road bike were tied a bundle of sticks he would use to mark out his way and record his journey.

Long's ride took him three days of largely non-stop cycling. He pedalled out of London, through Ely, Tring and Cambridge. He cycled along A roads and canal towpaths, along country tracks and across muddy fields. At sixteen locations along his route he drove one of his stakes into the ground. 'Starting from the entrance of St Martin's in London,' he later recalled:

and carrying the components of the sculpture strapped to my bicycle, I commenced a more-or-less continuous day-night-day-night cycle ride around the counties to the north of London, ending back at my flat in the East End. At random places and times along the way I left one part of the work at each place. Each consisted of a yellow painted vertical piece of wood stuck into the ground, with a blue horizontal cross-piece at the top. They were left in gardens, on verges or village greens, in fields etc.

Near the location of each stake Long attached a notice which his mother had typed for him on her typewriter. The notice read:

THIS IS ONE PART OF A PIECE OF SCULPTURE WHICH SURROUNDS AN AREA OF 2401 SQ. MILES. THERE ARE FIFTEEN OTHER SIMILAR PARTS, PLACED IRREGULARLY.

With this simple yet radical act Long broke free from the confines of the gallery, and from the con-straints of traditional sculpture. Long marked his progress and recorded his route on a map, which is all that's left of the work.

Originally Long's map was part of a triptych, locat-ing the local journey he'd made in progressively more abstract space: first in relation to an OS map of the area, then in relation to the country itself, and finally in the context of a map of the world. Much of Long's art is about reclamation. A few months before he made his cycling sculpture Long had hitchhiked from St Martin's back to his home in Bristol, stopping somewhere in the Wiltshire countryside before finding a field and walked up and down in the damp grass. He took a photograph of the resulting track, which he called *A Line Made by Walking*. He has been walking ever since – on moors, up mountains, over deserts and across the frozen glaciers of Antarctica – and you can tell. At sixty-nine, Long is lithe and energetic, a looming presence with the slightly weathered air of a country vet.

For most of his career Long has used natural materials to make his works, stones arranged on the floors of galleries or mud applied directly to the walls. In the 1970s he began making sculptures using River Avon mud – still his favoured material – and he's since become something of 'a mud expert'. With his walking works he reclaims the act of movement itself as a form of artistic activity. With his mud works he reclaims an elemental material. His cycling sculptures, which he's made several of over the years, reclaim the map as something in its own right: not as a reference to the world but as an abstract shape with some intrinsic beauty, suggesting but not describing the journey it describes. His work evokes the poetry of travel rather than its prose. Much of his art is about the spaces in between stopping points, about bodies and measurements, about moving through time and space and leaving traces of this movement only in faintly algebraic commemorations of the routes taken or the work done.

His subsequent work has occupied that fertile territory between an idea and its actualisation, between the act and its record. Often he documents his walking sculptures as maps, prints and photographs, narrating the story of them rather than reproducing the journeys themselves. Many of his walks are recorded only as text works, haiku-like prose poems, and talking to Long is a bit like encountering one of these enigmatic pieces. Underneath it all is an understanding that ideas can be beautiful in and of themselves. Long's *Cycling Sculpture, 1–3 December 1967* now only exists – perhaps only ever did exist – in map form. The shape marked out by the points he traced doesn't resolve into anything else. As a map it is vague, stripped of place-names, roads and topographical features. It is the record of a dreamt or unreal journey.

When I discovered Long's map I saw it as a challenge. I wanted to ride the route myself, to recreate the event of Long's journey, to see if I could experience what it might be like to turn a bicycle ride into a work of art. But I didn't quite know what the route the map described should be. When he made his sculpture the road system provided Long with his basic structure. The rest was inspired by what he described in a letter to me as a process of 'random attractiveness'. There was no forward planning. He was moved only by the environments he encountered to mark his arbitrary points on the map. 'I did not draw it or plan it first,' he wrote:

S C U L P T U R E   1ST–3RD DECEMBER 1967

Transported by bicycle and assembled at the
points shown on the map.   At each location
was placed a notice which read:

THIS IS ONE PART OF A PIECE OF SCULPTURE
WHICH SURROUNDS AN AREA OF 2401 SQ.MILES.
THERE ARE FIFTEEN OTHER SIMILAR PARTS,
PLACED IRREGULARLY.

ANY COMMENTS etc., TO:
RICHARD LONG,
31, FOURNIER STREET, LONDON E.1.

No photographs

or even mark it afterwards, – only the 'sculpture' points. I remember (in particular) empty fen roads, Ely cathedral & also passing <u>by chance</u>! Henry Moore's studio/village – Much Haddon? And the fire engines at the crash.

The Sculpture points were also 'random' but chosen for ease, practicality and to be fairly evenly spaced, one from another. They were always near or adjacent to the road.

Long's map was only half the story.

'The audacity of Long's early work,' writes the author Robert Macfarlane, 'lay in freeing sculpture from the constraints of scale. He dispersed his art into the landscape, busting it not just out of the gallery, but out of almost all spatial limits.' The mock-terse note on the signs he erected as part of *Cycling Sculpture, 1–3 December* is testament to this: 'No Photographs', a simple statement of fact. This was a sculpture it would be impossible to photograph, impossible to see, unless you went on your own journey around it. This was Long's great artistic realisation. 'I could make a piece of art which was 10 miles long,' he recalled in 1986, 'I could also make a sculpture which surrounded an area of 2,401 square miles […] by almost doing nothing, just walking and cycling.' The action formed the map but the artwork itself existed nowhere, somewhere in-between the ride and its record.

Many of his works are secret, unacknowledged, hidden. 'I like the idea,' he once told an interviewer, 'of making art almost from nothing or by doing almost nothing. It doesn't take a lot to turn ordinary things into art. It is enough to use stones as stones, for what they are.' Anonymity is key to much of what he does, but because of this subtlety his work re-enchants the world, making you read it in a new way. After exposure to Long's work you never quite know if that stone by the side of the road was left deliberately or is there by random chance. In a sense it doesn't really matter. 'I love that,' he has said, 'I love the idea that people might see a work of mine in the landscape, and that they might recognise it as human mark but not necessarily as a work of art. Let alone a work made by me. So often people find a circle of stones and think it might be a Richard Long. Other people can make my work for me.'

I wanted to leave London and follow Long's map, a map of empty space, a series of ghostly waypoints scattered across the landscape. It was October, the weather was warm and looked like it would hold for a last few days before the winter came. I thought I'd get a journey out of it − a structure emerging from the ride, connecting the dots. I wanted to leave the rutted runs of the courier-circuit behind. Long's project was too tempting to ignore: fifteen points making no reference to cities, to pick-ups and drop-offs, or to the landscape itself. The gravitational sling of London throwing you out before drawing you back in. Emptiness and the road.

I wondered if there would be any connection between my discoveries as a courier and Long's sense of the bicycle journey as art. I liked, too, the idea of a journey made not according to the dictates of controllers and clients, nor according to the tyranny of the *A–Z*, but within the looser confines of Long's map. And so I decided to emulate Long, to recreate *Cycling Sculpture*, to go on a circuit that would take a few days to complete and wouldn't end back where I began.

I overlaid the route over a map of Britain and plotted the rough course: out through Hertfordshire, through Aylesbury, Buckingham and Towcester. Then north through Cambridgeshire, bypassing Peterborough and Huntingdon, before heading north to Ely, marooned in its island in the fens, before turning south again for Cambridge, Newmarket and then down to Bishop's Stortford. It would be a long ride, quite different from the day job, giving me time to lose myself on the road. I'd do nothing else.

Before I set off, however, I wanted to speak to Long about his journey, to find out what he had to say about the bicycle ride not just as experience, but as art. So I sought him out. We met in the Magdala pub in Hampstead, famous as the place where Ruth Ellis shot her lover David Blakely in 1955, subsequently becoming the last woman to be hanged in Britain. You can still make out the bullet holes in the wall outside – faint traces, like Long's work, of historical events scored subtly into the surface of the world.

Though nearing seventy, Long is tall and lithe, with the enthusiastic, boyish air of a Scout Leader. He was wearing a nondescript anorak and sturdy walking boots. His eyebrows are the only unruly things about him, sprouting up over his forehead and giving his face a permanent expression of faint surprise.

Long said he couldn't remember much of the route of this, his first Cycling Sculpture, or of the journey itself. He remembered riding through Tring, and recalled passing Ely Cathedral in the dark during the small hours of the second morning of his ride. He remembered sleeping for a few hours in a shed by the side of the road, lying on piles of mangelwurzels and being woken by hundreds of rats that had emerged from the woodwork to nibble on them. He said he had received a single enquiry about his signs, from a man on whose lawn he'd placed one part of his sculpture. He couldn't remember what the man had asked him.

On the way back home through east London he remembered passing the smouldering aftermath of a car crash, with firemen cutting someone out of their car with acetone torches. 'The smell was unbeliev-able,' he recalled, 'burning rubber, thick black smoke. I think there was blood on the road, and I just whizzed by on my bike.'

The idea of the piece, he told me, was to create a sculpture bigger than any other: to create a sculpture that could not be viewed all in one go, couldn't be consumed from one single vantage point, that resisted the tyranny of the gaze. The idea of the work was to be bigger than the reality. The piece was part of a body of work that played with scale. Long had once erected a sculpture on the top of Kilimanjaro, telling the papers that he'd created the world's highest sculpture. 'For some reason they didn't consider it newsworthy,' he told me. 'Really it's the shape itself that was important,' he said of *Cycling Sculpture, 1–3 December*, 'you could do the same ride anywhere, move the markers, place it over a map of London. The actual landscape I travelled over is unimportant.'

Long's art is founded on the traces left by the body in motion, but in its making it is also about the enjoyment of the body, and this he associates with his own childhood pursuits and interests. The joy of bodily exertion I'd discovered as a courier he'd applied to the making of art. 'Lots of people make art out of anguish,' he says, 'I make mine out of pleasure.' As a boy he'd always been a walker and a cyclist. His parents met because they were both members of a rambling club, and at school he was the captain of the cross-country running club.

He's often misread as a romantic artist, or as a political radical of some kind. I asked him if there was anything of the activist about his work – suggesting as it does ideas of right-to-roam and open access – but he told me he was an 'art animal, not a political animal'. He does, however, draw a distinction between his work and that of the American land artists, who use bulldozers and earthmovers to shape their environments to their will. His work isn't interventionist in quite that way. 'I'm not interested in imposing myself on the world,' he said.

Stories do seem central to his practice: the story of his own body moving through space and time, the story of the marks he makes as he goes, but he resists over-investing in the idea of art as a form of narrative. 'I don't have any great grand theories of walking, or of making art into a journey,' he told me later, 'they just seemed like good ideas at the time.' Though the backdrops to his journeys – mountains, forests and deserts – are often beautiful, they are largely irrelevant, or, if not irrelevant, a happy outcome of the pieces he makes. Instead he talks enthusiastically about technicalities and practicalities. Of the making of *Road River*, a meandering line of paint he dripped onto the tarmac of Box Hill in Surrey, to be ridden over by the road cyclists during the 2012 London Olympics, he said, 'we had to use biodegradable paint. And we had to do it overnight, and the paint would dry very quickly.' He's interested in what he has done rather than in why he has done it.

Outside the pub, as we were leaving, he examined my bicycle. 'A track bike?' he asked. 'That's a strange choice.' He asked me who I thought would win the Tour. 'Chris Froome's looking good,' I said.

'He is,' said Long. 'Well, never meet your heroes,' he said, as he smiled and stalked away back up the hill.

Richard Long, *Road River* (2012)

I left the next day, at first light. London fell away grad-
ually and I never really knew when I'd moved beyond
it. After a while the city gave way to suburbia, to the
monolithic headquarters of medium-sized companies,
to traffic depots and mysterious sidings by the motor-

way, to increasing rural paranoia. There were signs on fences reading 'Country Watch operates here'. The roads altered too, out here, roughing themselves up, clad in a firmer asphalt covering the better to resist the trials of winter.

The ride took me three days. I wanted to exhaust myself in the recreation. I didn't stop to take notes, and I now remember the journey only as a litany of events, sequences stitched together by the rhythms of the bicycle. Like some of Long's 'text works', in which he simply lists the actions he performed during one of his journeys, in the end I was left with just a sequence of names – towns I had glided through in the October sunshine, unnamed copses I camped in as night fell. I remember fragments, frozen scenes from a steady stream of images: Halloween decorations; hobby-farmers selling squashes by the side of the road. Honey at £4 a lb. Eggs £1.20 per half dozen. Hertfordshire, 'County of Opportunity', signs to a nearby Hare Krishna temple. A canal towpath by a fishing lake with a huge fibreglass dinosaur peering over the fence. A lake with signs announcing the presence of a malignant shrimp invader: 'wash your tackle in the fresh water provided'. Dead badger roadkill, squirrel parchment, stoats, pigeons and tits, all squashed into the tarmac.

I moved down unmarked roads, roads that didn't appear on any map, the products of the expansion of satellite towns with their branded mottos: 'air to breathe, space to think, room to grow.' I placed my first post and sign on a telegraph pole outside Aylesbury, above a poster for the 'Cirque Normandie: the spectacle magnifique'. After that I lost track of where I placed them: in fields, on embankments by the side of roads, in the middle of village greens. No one seemed to notice. No one stopped me.

At Silverstone, stinkpot mushrooms pushed through the boy-racer tempered tarmac. It was sunny, the mist had burnt off. Everything was geared toward the car round here: the racetrack itself was a monument to automobility. Cars rushed past.

I slept in a copse outside Northampton, listening to the cries of pheasants as the sun went down. Later they were replaced with the hoots of owls. I listened to the fizzing of a power line, hearing the surge in the grid as a million homes made tea before dying down to a gentle hum as people went to sleep. A gamekeeper had left a necklace of dead corvids – crows and jays – hanging from a fence in the clearing. A shooting platform sprouted from the trees overlooking a blue-barrel feeding station for the pecking pheasants. This was John Clare country, I slept near the asylum in which he was incarcerated for four years before he absconded and walked north to find his lost love.

On the morning of the second day I was woken by sunrise coming over the tops of the trees. I pedalled on through the frigid air, stopping for coffee in Rushdon, erecting further signs as I went, in Peterborough and Ely, and then turned south for Cambridge.

Long was a better rider, fitter than me perhaps, or more dedicated to his journey, un-weighed down by tent and sleeping bag. He was freer, too, unburdened by the desire to recreate a journey, he simply had to make one. He pushed on through the night, sleeping only when fatigue struck. My ride was more domestic, and on the second night I sought out a bed in Pampisford, on the outskirts of Cambridge. It was an appropriate staging post. Before we left Cambridge my host, a Fellow of Jesus College, showed me one of Long's other works in the senior common room. It was a mural of muddy hand-prints spread in a circle, a mandala, hypnotically uniform apart from the slight variations in the splash at the fingertips. He told me that someone had once wiped away two of the muddy fingerprints from the light switch in the corner of the room. When the Fellows wrote to Long and asked him what to do he sent them a phial of Avon mud, sanctified by the artist, and instructed them to recreate it with their own hands.

We left Cambridge along the 'DNA trail', a bike path made up of 10,257 coloured tiles mapping out the nucleotides of the BRCA2 gene. The gene is responsible for susceptibility to breast cancer, and was discovered at the nearby Sanger Institute. The route felt like another, grimmer kind of mapping – the mapping of the fragile body. We picked our way through the technolands which surround the city, an idyll of the suburban planner's pen. The sun blazed. The country was full of signs telling you what not to do: 'No cold calling'; 'Countrywatch'; 'Say no to the Wind Farm'.

I slept well and left Pampisford at dawn. Damsons and blackberries flicked by in the hedgerows. Birds I didn't know the names of sang in the fields. I arrived back in London in the afternoon. The pull of the city was strong. Following the River Lea I passed a big bus depot and a taxi rank, serving the city from its satellite towns. I sat by the river and watched the fronds moving in the stream. A sparrow hawk broke in front of me. I passed canal boats and barges, watched over by the huge warehouses, workshops, gasometers and pylons, and sheds as big as churches, ringing the M25.

I came in to London alongside Springfield marina as the storm clouds were gathering over Hackney Marshes. The wind showered conkers, scattered leaves from the trees, signalling the end of summer. I cycled past the mothballed velodrome in the Olympic park, past narrowboats on the river. I placed my last sign on the side of a path under a great willow tree before I rode back in to the city. My ring of signs, I hoped, was still intact.

6

– On the Road –

And I rose up and knew I was tired
and I continued my journey.
– Edward Thomas

W hen winter arrives the work of the cycle courier becomes much less rewarding, despite the
fact that you earn a bit more money. The fair-weather
riders who swell the ranks in the summer and compete
for jobs, squeezing earnings, fall away by late autumn.
Standing by becomes a torture. You pray for work, not
just so that you earn money but so that you can keep
warm. Your toes freeze. Your joints seize up. When it
rains the rain mixes with dirt and grime and wicks its
way across your body. The fine London dust, a lethal
composite of heavy metals, uncracked hydrocarbons
and other killer particles, seeps into your pores and
stains your bathwater grey. By the end of a working
day you wear the city. Grit-bearded and fume-lunged,
your fingers are covered in dark tarmacadam shadows.
The roads empty of other cyclists. Bicycles are pickled
in the salt and the grit.

In *In Pursuit of Spring*, an account of a bicycle ride
he made from London to the Quantock Hills, the poet

Edward Thomas claimed that 'many days in London have no weather. We are aware only that it is hot or cold, dry or wet; that we are in or out of doors; that we are at ease or not.' But after three years on the road I knew this not to be true. During the winter I had come to attend to the weather every morning as carefully as a sailor about to put to sea.

After a while on the circuit some couriers get itchy feet. They want travel, to get away from it all. They want to cycle around the world, or to race, or to go and ride L'Étape du Tour, the amateur event in which non-professionals are allowed to ride a stage of the Tour de France on closed roads. I had more modest ambitions. They say you can only really consider yourself a proper courier after you've worked for three winters. It was my third winter on the circuit, my third year of shuffling packages around the indifferent city. I was growing weary of it. I had begun to think of the future. Couriering had provided a good stopgap in between studying for various degrees. They had racked up along with the miles ridden – BA, MA, PhD – but I had reached the end of that particular treadmill too. My girlfriend had found out she was pregnant, and I wasn't sure cycle couriering was the best way to support this new life. It was time to move on.

In 1913, one hundred years earlier, Thomas had felt similarly stifled by the city. *In Pursuit of Spring* begins as an urban journey. It is written from the perspective of what he called 'Clapham Junction Man', a figure embodying many of his own anxieties about the corrupting forces of urban life. 'In the streets, for the present,' Thomas wrote:

the roar continued of the inhuman masses of humanity, amidst which a child's crying for a toy was an impertinence, a terrible pretty interruption of the violent moving swoon. Between the millions and the one no agreement was visible.

If Long's ride was an exploration, Thomas's was an escape, taking him away from London and towards the villages of an England he felt was being lost forever. It was a to be a ride through 'Nether Stowey, Kilver, Crowcombe, and West Bagborough, to the high point where the Taunton-Bridgwater road tops the hills and shows all Exmoor behind, all the Mendips before, and upon the left the sea, and Wales very far off.' It was a journey made 'on or with a bicycle', Thomas wrote, and 'the season was Easter, a March Easter'. For Thomas the journey represented a way of leaving it all behind – leaving the stresses of the hack journalism by which he made his living and escaping from the anonymous masses of the city. *In Pursuit of Spring* was to be his last prose work.

Thomas's litany of unfamiliar names was too attractive to ignore. Like him, I wanted to leave London behind again, to go on a longer journey than Long's ride. I wanted to seek Spring on the road. The centenary coincidence was tempting. And so on Good

Friday, one hundred years after him – and during the coldest March for fifty years – I set off by bicycle in pursuit of Thomas, to ride the roads he'd ridden along and see what of the route had changed, and what had remained the same.

Thomas's journey was part of a trend, born of the growing affordability of bicycles at the turn of the twentieth century, of going on cycling tours in order to discover the countryside on your own terms. In 1924 the journalist and keen cyclist C. E. Montague had set off on a similar journey, a twenty-four hour bicycle ride from Manchester to Charing Cross, the point from which distances to London are traditionally measured. He embarked on his journey, he wrote, in order to 'make friends with a great trunk road.'

Truly to know a country, Montague thought (and here he was in agreement with Thomas), it was not enough to have seen it only in isolated chunks: to have glimpsed it through train windows as you were whipped along the rails, or to have encountered it slowly, at the plodding, drawn-out pace of pedestrian speed. 'By car the thing would be easy', he went on, 'but then travel by car is only semi-travel, verging on the demi-semi-travel that you get in trains.' To truly know a road, Montague continued, you must feel it 'with your muscles, as well as see it, before even your eyes can get a full sense of it.'

The new velocities provided by car and train travel that Montague was reacting against had bent the world around themselves, influencing the way it looked as well as what it felt like. The tyranny of cars meant that roads would increasingly be built straight and wide. As cars came to dominate, advertisers had to simplify their designs so that posters could be read from vehicles travelling at previously unimagined speeds. And as travel became ever quicker and cheaper, anxieties set in over how the new ways of travelling were isolating people from the places they inhabited.

Different modes of transport have their own rhythms and their own vernacular. Driving isolates, cocooning you in the car's aluminium embrace and throwing up vistas on the windshield as though they were projections on a screen. Train-travel frames the world and smoothes out its idiosyncrasies. Rails cut through the landscape on the paths of least resistance, both economic and geological, divorcing travellers from topography as they're rushed along the tracks. Underground, on the tube, commuters are removed from the landscape still further. Differences in journeys registered only in the acoustic signatures of the lines – their particular hums and rattles – and the time they take to complete.

Montague's journey, like Thomas's, was a way of reclaiming speed. For him cycling was the perfect compromise between the tyranny of the automobile and the slowness of walking. The bike allowed him to feel the grain of a landscape whilst still providing an efficient means of travelling through it. It gave Montague a new and intimate way of experiencing his own country, the warp and weft of the land, the texture of roads, the intimate geography of an England he felt was changing forever.

Montague's and Thomas's journeys were also quests for a sense of national identity. Britain never had as strong a bicycle road racing tradition as did Continental Europe, but in the early twentieth century the bicycle still contributed to conceptions of nationhood. The journey across the South Downs undertaken by the draper's assistant Hoopdriver in H. G. Wells's novel *The Wheels of Chance*, in which he encounters flirtatious women and angry vicars, is typical of the narratives of the mass-mobilisation of the cycling middle classes that were popular before the First World War. In the late nineteenth and early twentieth century, freed by their bikes, clerks and shop assistants could finally leave the city under their own steam and return home within a day. Cycling clubs proliferated, offering their members the chance to go 'rambling on wheels' and connect with the land in a way they had previously been unable to.

Almost as soon as it was invented the bicycle was enthusiastically endorsed as a means of teaching people the contours of their own country. 'The countryside was obviously a real geographical space before bicyclists travelled to it in the 1890s,' writes the cycling historian Zack Furness, but it 'was also produced by the act of cycling.' As a newspaper report from the time had it:

Our high pressure, our covetous greed of the minute, have placed the bicycle upon the road in its thousands; and out of evil there has in this way come good, for it is to the green country that the fevered youth of the nation race, with rustling rubber and sharp-sounding bell. As they rush through the air and flash past the village and field, *there is borne in upon them the educational germ of a love for landscape*; they see, and they cannot help noting, the contrast between smoke-grimed cities and 'fresh woods and pastures new.'

Cycling, like walking, can be a subversive act. Unlike walking, however, it depends on infrastructure – on the network of macadamised roads which spidered out over the country in the nineteenth century, coming into being alongside the rise of the *flâneur*. After the railways began to dominate travel it was thought that roads would become redundant; that they'd whither away through want of use, and that in the future both freight and people would be carried exclusively by rail, and a decade or so before Thomas embarked on his ride, the bicycle had yet to make its mark as a machine for touring, stymied by the bad roads and green lanes of the countryside.

However, in 1901 Edgar Hooley, a surveyor for Nottinghamshire County, was out walking in Derbyshire when he came upon a stretch of road smoother than any he'd seen before. He asked the locals how they'd achieved such a good surface and they told him it was an accident: a barrel of tar had spilt on the road and, in an attempt to soak it up, they had poured on slag from the local coal mine. Hooley stole the idea and patented his tarmac process later that year, and the first tarmacadam roads in England were built in 1902.

The new roads were quickly seized upon by cyclists. In Hilaire Belloc's *The Stane Street*, in many ways a companion volume to *In Pursuit of Spring* and published in the same year, Belloc (who rode a high-Wheeler and was for a time cycling correspondent for the *Pall Mall Gazette*) wrote about the 'deep time' implicit in the road network that was being challenged by the metalling of the nation's roads. England's road system, he wrote:

has not been planned. It has developed in the main by the gradual hardening and metalling and improving of the old green lanes: hence the peculiar narrowness and tortuousness of the English road system as we have it to-day.

England's highways offered a rebuke to the delirious and rigorously planned grid-systems of the new world, laid out in cities like New York. For Belloc they represented the memory of a race. The old trade routes corresponded with a sense of identity that, Belloc felt, was being quickly eroded.

By 1922, most London roads were surfaced with wood, first used to dampen down the noise of passing traffic outside hospitals, later used as the surface of choice across the network. The favoured wood was Jarra, a dense hardwood prized for its hardwearing qualities. It was imported from Australia and soaked in kerosene to make it tougher, but the process made it prone to catching fire. After floods or heavy rainfall it would often warp and bend, destroying the road surface. Roads in the suburbs, on the other hand, were generally still made of crushed stone and dirt.

Certain kinds of roads, the kind Thomas loved best, wear their monumental wear on their surfaces, registering the passing of time in their shape, their depth, their very names. In the countryside Holloways, formed by the tramping of thousands of feet – both human and animal – have been formed by travel in quite direct ways. Robert Macfarlane argues that such records of travel can be 'humbling, for they are landmarks that speak of habit rather than suddenness. Trodden by innumerable feet, cut by innumerable wheels, they are the records of journeys made to market, to worship, to sea.'

I'd found that such stark reminders of travel were rare in London, whose roads are never more than a few months old, left crisscrossed with the scars of numerous face-lifts. In the city asphalt is shed annually, like the skin of a snake: scraped off with flailing chains before being spat out into waiting trucks and laid anew by machines which resemble urban combine harvesters. Asphalt suffers from an amnesia unknown to mud and stone. 'Deserted roads', as Thomas Hardy wrote, 'bespeak a tomb-like stillness more emphatic than that of glades and pools.' Roads were memorials, I realised as I rode around London. Empty roads are a theatre stage waiting to be animated. And yet despite their cyclical renewal, many roads possess a simple identity borne of their shape, an identity that can only be discovered by finding out what it feels like to ride them. In this my recreation of Thomas's ride felt like a way of recreating a memory. His book was one record of the journey, the official record, but in recreating it I thought I might understand something about his writing too. I hoped that, out on the road, I might discover its source.

Though many of the roads Thomas took are now unfriendly to cyclists, I wanted to follow his route as closely as possible, and so I set off on my own journey from his house on Shelgate Road in Clapham. To find Spring he first had to struggle through the newly-built suburbs of London. 'The suburban by-streets already looked rideable', he noted on the first day of his ride, 'but they were false prophets [...] the surface between the west end of Nightingale Lane and the top of Burntwood Lane was fit only for fancy cycling.'

For Thomas roads were entities, monuments

to travel. According to de Selby, the scientist savant whose presence haunts, via footnotes, Flann O'Brien's *The Third Policeman*, roads are 'the most ancient of human monuments, surpassing by many tens of centuries the oldest thing of stone that man has reared to mark his passing. The tread of time [...] levelling all else, has beaten only to a more enduring hardness the pathways that have been made throughout the world.' Cyclists recognise the monumentality of roads better than most. For drivers the road is merely, as Iain Sinclair writes, a 'dull silvertop that acts as a prophylactic between driver and landscape', but over time cyclists develop an asphalt consciousness drawn from years of minute observation conducted from the saddle. In his 1885 treatise 'Physiologie de l'asphalte', Alexis Martin described the way in which asphalt, then a relatively new element in urban life, was beginning to be read in various ways by city dwellers. 'The manufacturer passes over the asphalt conscious of its quality,' he wrote:

the old man searches it carefully, follows it just as long as he can, happily taps his cane so the wood resonates, and recalls with pride that he personally witnessed the laying of the first sidewalks; the poet walks on it pensive and unconcerned, muttering lines of verse; the stockbroker hurries past, calculating the advantages of the last rise in wheat.

Thomas was a great aficionado of roads, of their surfaces and gradients and of what it felt like to travel

along them. In 'The Path' he described a track 'winding like silver', worn into the woods by children who,
'With the current of their feet' create a monument to
their passing. In his poem 'Roads' he wrote:

> I love roads:
> The goddesses that dwell
> Far along invisible
> Are my favourite gods.

In *In Pursuit of Spring* he pays as much attention
to the individual character of the roads he travels over
as to the birds, rivers and trees that he passes on his
way. The book is a catalogue of pathways, an encyclopaedia of the surfaces of travel. In it he describes roads
'as straight and sharp as a hog's back'; roads 'heavy
and wet'; roads like living things, steaming as they dry
in the sun. Roads and paths were for him symbols of
common life, figured as democratic spaces. They were
marked out by the slap of time and the unconscious
dictates of collective movement.

On his way out of London Thomas recorded that he
shared the road with 'a few genial muscular Christians
with their daughters, and equally genial muscular ag-
nostics with no children; bands of scientifically-minded
ramblers with knickerbockers, spectacles, and cameras.' Picking my way through Wandsworth, Tooting and

Morden in the cold March air I was accompanied only by cars speeding to beat the Easter weekend rush and the odd muttering walker or jogger. I passed through Morden by the banks of the Wandle, once Nelson's favourite trout stream, then for many years a grubby industrial river, now reclaimed by the Wandle Trust, who fish shopping trolleys out of it at weekends and have recently restocked it with trout.

Middle England was washing its caravans as I crossed Surrey, and when I got to Epsom, a crowd was crucifying a portly Jesus in the square. 'Kill him! Crucify him!' they yelled enthusiastically. I sat at a sandwich shop called the 'Green Machine' and ate a bacon sandwich as a man addressed the crowds. Across the square, the crucifixion continued. There were hymns. The sun came out and warmed my back.

On the way out of town flags of St George fluttered in the cold wind. A 'VOTE UKIP' sign hung from a tree. I crossed the M25 by a footbridge and looked down at the traffic surging around London. I felt I might have broken free from its centripetal pull, but the roads felt much the same. Outside the White Horse pub further on I spotted a pair of stocks. They felt like a warning. Thomas's England was, a year before war was declared, similarly suspicious of outsiders. At Bradford on Avon he noted an election poster reading 'Foreigners tax us; let us tax them.' The Gypsies and Travellers that Thomas observed camping on common land all along his route have today been brushed away under motorway bypasses or onto brownfield sites. The entrances to pitchable land are blocked with concrete blocks.

A few miles through Surrey I found and climbed Box Hill, famous in Thomas's day as a picturesque picnicking spot. Now it's a Mecca for cyclists who come to test their calves against its inclines. Box Hill featured in the 2012 Olympic cycling road race, and the surface of Zig Zag Lane, which winds seductively up it, is a model of macadamed perfection. There were signs painted on the road 'Cav for PM!'; 'Victory Ahead', with the tell-tale splash and splatter of the paint giving them away as guerrilla jobs. Some were probably left over from the Games.

Half way up I encountered Richard Long's *Road River*, a meandering line of white road paint, a schizophrenic road marking which echoed the exaggerated, almost comic meanders of Zig Zag Lane itself. I counted 37 Surrey MAMILS go past as I sat and looked at Long's sculpture. Cars climbed the hill too. Some drivers shouted things at the cyclists as they passed. Most of the cyclists didn't look up or acknowledge me. Instead they concentrated on their own suffering, concentrated on trying to climb this hill slightly faster than they ever had before.

After a while it began to get cold, so I left the hill and re-joined Thomas's route. I skirted the Hog's Back, which Thomas described as 'a road fit for the herald Mercury, and the other gods, because it is as much in heaven as on earth'. Now it's the vicious A31, not a pleasant road to cycle on, so I travelled along its flank and continued through Farnham, entering Hampshire through Alton, Chawton and Alresford. Chawton, Thomas records, 'is well aware of the fact that Jane Austen once dwelt in a house at the fork there', and now the 'Jane Austen heritage trail' is clearly sign-posted, leading you through a dingy underpass below the A31 to her cottage.

Though Thomas noted the literary associations of the places he travelled through, he wasn't particularly interested in the past. He wrote mainly as a passive cataloguer of nature and of the people he met, punctu-ating this stream of observation with disquisitions on such things as the decline of clay pipe smoking and the inability of civilisation to produce a decent set of waterproofs.

I stayed the night in Farnham and woke early the next day. I left with the sunrise and climbed out of Middle-bourne onto the Hampshire hills. A torn up porno mag was scattered in the hedgerow by a stream, ripe pinks and reds glinting obscenely through the leaves. The sun came out at Winchester. At Itchen Abbot I stopped, walked down to the river on a footpath that ran across a bridge and through a garden alongside a private stretch of river, where I had lunch. Huge gray-ling flicked themselves around the stream.

I passed East Dean and West Dean, below the shadow of the Dean escarpment, which is still much as Thomas describes it, 'Dotted with Yew, that is seen running parallel to the railway, a quarter of a mile away.' At East Grimstead I met Malcolm, a farmer who was battling cockchafers in the churchyard. His eyes streamed continually from the cold as spoke. His family farm overlooked the churchyard, but he'd given it up now, he said. Five generations at least had worked that farm before him. His wife was from the same village, and his father and grandfather would both have been alive when Thomas passed through.

Malcolm still kept a few sheep, he said, which he used to keep the grass down on the land over the ridge I'd just passed. It made up some of the oldest yew forest in these parts. He was proud of the land: 'a fierce patriot'. He was against the EU. 'Can't even bury your dead sheep on the farm anymore.' He had written to his MEP about disposing of dead sheep but his letter had been ignored. The cockchafers were tough, he said, but he thought he was making progress. 'I've dug wider holes this year,' he said, 'seeing as you can't buy anything strong enough to kill them anymore.'

That night I slept for twelve hours straight in a friend's house nestled in the Wiltshire hills. My friend was away and had left the key out for me, but I'd forgotten to buy provisions on my way in and the closest village was too far to ride back to after a day in the saddle. I drank whisky and ate cheese because I had nothing else. Guinea fowl patrolled the lawns. A wire rabbit sculpture prayed to the setting sun.

I woke to bright dawn. A hawk was sunning itself on a fence post at the end of the garden. The world had been transformed during the night, from overcast to frosty and brilliantly bright. Ice flamed and flickered in the ditches.

The dirt roads that ran behind the house were hard going, frozen ditches and crackling frost. I stopped and pushed my bike often. Eventually the old farm tracks gave way to tarmac, to the most perfect cycling road. I slipped through this tree-lined tunnel in a blur, the wind whipping tears from my eyes. The rocket-like spire of Salisbury Cathedral flickered through the trees to my right. Pigeons and pheasants broke around me, following me along the road. A hawk flapped into the air. In the distance I could hear the faint pop-pop of shotgun fire.

I arrived in Salisbury as the bells were striking ten, but I left almost immediately to cross Salisbury Plain. The Plain has since before Thomas's time been a military training area, and hasn't been developed much at all. The vast expanses of it fell away in every direction. The sun was beaming down, but a cold wind blew at my back. Just before I arrived in West Levington, I came across a plaque:

At this spot Mr. Dean of Imber was attacked and Robbed by Four Highwaymen, in the evening of October 21st 1839. After a spirited pursuit of three hours one of the Felons BEN-JAMIN COLCLOUGH fell Dead on Chitterne Down. THOMAS SAUNDERS, GEORGE WATERS & RICH-ARD HARRIS, were eventually Captured and convicted at the ensuing Quarter Sessions at Devizes, and Transported for the term of Fifteen Years. This Monument is erected by Public Subscription as a warning to those who presumptuously think to escape the punishment God has threatened against Thieves and Robbers.

Outside Steeple Ashton, I found a sparrowhawk freshly killed by a car. I put it in my pocket, hoping to find a more fitting grave than this roadside verge outside a caravan park. Stopping for lunch at a muddy fishing lake, I buried the bird under some ivy. Carp fishermen sat around the pond, using their Easter Sunday wisely, whistling to each other and catching nothing while I was there. Bullrushes bent in the wind.

The fourth day was colder, overcast. I rode back up the Avon along the side of a valley, along a canal towpath that ran parallel to the railway and to the river. It was lined with canal boats from many of which wood smoke was just emerging. Unfriendly joggers passed me. My cold hands were juddered by the bad surface of the track until I hit the good roads again, before attacking a series of hard climbs into the Mendips, where the earth had become bright red.

It was easy going from Wells, across the Somerset Levels, wondrous and strange and empty, with dykes running across the crest of the land. I couldn't see the horizon for the cloud. Glastonbury Tor stood above me, overlooking it all. I sailed rather than cycled across the Levels, using the strong winds to tack along the best roads. For a while I watched two ravens harry a buzzard. Pylons all converged on Glastonbury. I skirted Shepton Mallet, and at Chezdoy some dogs chased me, barking through the wind.

One of Thomas's last stopping points was at Nether Stowey, sometime home of his great hero Samuel Taylor Coleridge. Though Coleridge's cottage was bought by the National Trust in 1909, Thomas couldn't get inside. Now you're encouraged to sit by the fire next to which Coleridge wrote 'Frost at Midnight' and poke at the embers. It wasn't an auspicious end to my ride. 'Nether Stowey offered no temptations to be compared with those of the road leading out of it,' wrote Thomas, and I tended to agree.

After a while I left and headed back towards Taunton via Cothelstone hill, the summit of the Quantocks, where Thomas had concluded his own ride. It was a stiff climb along a dirt track. A bin overflowed with plastic bags full of dogshit. I sat at the windswept top next to the seven sisters, the rocky foundations of a long-destroyed folly, on a log bench much like that which Thomas describes in *In Pursuit of Spring*. There were views over the hills, and out over the sea to Wales. The wind howled at my back. I ate Kendal mint cake, which I'd bought in the gift shop at Coleridge's cottage, while peewits cried about me. There was still no sign of Spring.

7

– Coda: Breaking Away –

*I*n *Pursuit of Spring* was a forward-looking book. Telegraph poles thrum through Thomas's arcadia as regularly as oaks and elms; the sounds of factories and city life are just as present as birdsong. Railways run beside the roads and canals he describes along his way. In 1913 his roads, he recorded, were 'travelled by an occasional (but not sufficiently occasional) motor car'. The car was a warning, but also something to be documented: a premonition of an automobile-centric future. 'Is this not the awakening of England?' he concluded, a question that wasn't entirely rhetorical.

Yet one thing of the near future he didn't mention was the war. In *In Pursuit of Spring* he ignores the fortifications installed at Box Hill and Guildford in anticipation of invasion. He mentions the military encampments which still occupy Salisbury Plain, but offers no further comment on them. Perhaps it was a wilful lapse, for he surely knew what was coming. He was killed during the first day of the battle of Arras, on Easter Monday, 1917, four years, almost to the day, after he made his journey. His heart was stopped by the pressure-wave of a shell that also stopped his watch, yet left no mark on his body.

My pursuit of Thomas's Spring was to be my last

journey while working as a courier. Not long after I returned from the Quantocks I gave up the job. It was never, for me, a long-term proposition. Many of the riders I knew over thirty began to regret it. After three years, they warned me, you can't get away. You forget you ever knew how to do anything else. 'Leave while you still can.' It was a warning written on their bodies. Some of the older riders looked as though they were falling to pieces. The work had taken its toll. Knees start to creak, legs seize up. Skin, weathered by the city's mercilessness, tightens about the skull. After a while it seemed as if their bicycles were the only things keeping these riders together. Their bikes were functioning as prostheses, as mineral skeletons, ensuring that their legs kept spinning and their arms continued their twitching dance over the tarmac. It was a future which frightened me. I didn't want to become a donkey, a long-term career courier, and so, that Spring, on returning from the Quantocks, I gave up my life on the road.

I still dream of the job, for it taught me a lot. In his memoir *The Bicycle Rider in Beverly Hills*, William Saroyan describes his early love affair with the bicycle as a form of literary and moral education. 'On the way,' he writes:

I found out all the things without which I could never be the writer I am. I was not yet sixteen when I understood a great deal, from having ridden bicycles for so long, about style, speed, grace, purpose, value, form, integrity, health, humor, music, breathing and finally and perhaps best, of the relationship between the beginning and the end.

I felt bicycle couriering had given me a similar education. As a courier the ride I loved best was the last of the day, the ride home, when your legs had gone through weariness, stiffness and fatigue, and finally felt unburdened: light and easy. Then you felt like you weren't riding the bike but being drawn along with it. Once the day was done you got a burst of speed, a home coming rush that willed you on and made you forget your tiredness. Freed of the need to conserve anything for a possible final rush-job, you let yourself go.

I still cycle daily, but I never really get that feeling any more. Now my commute to work – along the Lea Bridge Road (past club riders heading in the opposite direction, escaping London), through Hackney Marshes and Dalston, along the Essex Road and up the side of the Pentonville escarpment by Angel, and then down through the basin of the valley of the river Fleet and onto the Strand – is a meditative one, dulled and deadened by repetition. I have become a gentler cyclist too. I no longer run red lights or buzz pedestrians at crossings. I no longer race in alleycat races. I miss the work, but I'm glad I'm no longer a courier. I've heeded the warning of Flann O'Brien's Atomic Theory, and of Jarry's contracted racers who rode themselves to death. Though the wheels still turn, I'd learnt enough from the job. I got out while I still could.

– References –

1 Prologue

Bella Bathurst, *The Bicycle Book* (2011)

Charles Baudelaire, 'The Painter of Modern Life' (1859)

Walter Benjamin, *The Arcades Project* (1999)

Michel De Certeau, *The Practice of Everyday Life* (1984)

Guy Debord, *Society   the Spectacle* (1977)

— 'Theory of the Dérive' in the *Situationist International Anthology* (2006)

Paul Fournel, *Need for the Bike* (2003)

David Herlihy, *Bicycle* (2004)

Patrick Keiller, *The View from the Train: Cities and Other Landscapes* (2013)

Valeria Luiselli, *Sidewalks* (2014)

V. S Pritchett, *London Perceived* (1962)

Jonathan Raban, *Soft City* (1974)

Steen Eiler Rasmussen, *London: the Unique City I* (1934)

Graham Robb, *The Discovery of France* (2007)

Iain Sinclair, *Lights Out for the Territory* (1997)

Sukhdev Sandhu, *Nighthaunts: A Journey through the London Night* (2007)

Matt Seaton, *The Escape Artist* (2002)

Rebecca Solnit, *Wanderlust: A History of Walking* (2001)

— *A Field Guide to Getting Lost* (2006)

2 Circulation

Nicholas Barton, *The Lost Rivers of London* (1962)

Charles Bukowski, *Post Office* (1971)

William Gibson, *Virtual Light* (1993)

Charles G. Harper, *The Brighton Road: The Classic Highway to the South* (1892)

Henry Miller, *Tropic of Capricorn* (1957)

Jeffrey L. Kidder, *Urban Flow: Bike Messengers and the City* (2011)

Thomas Pynchon, *The Crying of Lot 49* (1965)

Will Self, *The Quantity Theory of Insanity* (1991)

Ken Worpole, *Staying Close to the River* (1995)

Patrick Wright, *A Journey Through Ruins* (1991)

3 Cartesian Centaurs

Luigi Bartolini, *Bicycle Thieves* (1946)

Samuel Beckett, *More Pricks Than Kicks* (1934)

— *Mercier and Camier* (1970)

Alastair Brotchie, *Alfred Jarry: A Pataphysical Life* (2011)

Gregory J. Downey, *Telegraph Messenger Boys: Labor, Technology, and Geography 1850–1950* (2002)

John Foot, *Pedelare! Pedelare!* (2011)

Ford Madox Ford, *The Soul of London: A Survey of a Modern City* (1905)

James Heartfield, 'Lodonostalgia' in *Blueprint* (2004)

Alfred Jarry, *The Supermale* (1964)

— *The Selected Works of Alfred Jarry* (1965)

Hugh Kenner, *Samuel Beckett: A Critical Study* (1961)

Joe Kerr and Andrew Gibson (eds.), *London from Punk to Blair* (2003)

Henry Mayhew, *London Labour and the London Poor* (1851)

Flann O'Brien, *The Third Policeman* (1966)

George Orwell, *Down and Out in Paris and London* (1933)

4 Race

Roland Barthes, *What is Sport?* (2007)

— 'The Tour de France as Epic' in *Mythologies* (2012)

Richard Cobb, *Tour de France* (1976)

Graeme Fife, *The Beautiful Machine* (2008)

Tim Krabbé, *The Rider* (2002)

Christopher S. Thompson, *The Tour de France: A Cultural History* (2006)

James Waddington, *Bad to the Bone* (1998)

Geoffrey Wheatcroft, *Le Tour: A History of the Tour de France* (2003)

5 Off the Map

Walter Benjamin, 'A Berlin Chronicle' in *Walter Benjamin: Selected Writings* (2005)

William Fotheringham, *Put Me Back on My Bike: In Search of Tom Simpson* (2007)

Simon Garfield, *On The Map: Why the world looks the way it does* (2012)

Nigel Henderson, *Photographs of Bethnal Green 1949–1952* (1978)

— *References* —

Richard Long, *Heaven and Earth* (2009)

R. W. Mylne, *London and its Environs, Topographical and Geological* (1856)

Nick Papadimitriou, *Scarp* (2013)

Dieter Roelstraete, *Richard Long: A Line Made by Walking* (2010)

Iain Sinclair, *American Smoke* (2013)

— *London Orbital* (2003)

— *Edge of The Orison* (2005)

— 'The Raging Peloton' in the *London Review of Books* (2011)

— *Hackney, that Rose-Red Empire, A Confidential Report* (2009)

Ben Tufnell (ed.), *Richard Long: Selected Statements and Interviews* (2007)

6 On the Road

Hilaire Belloc, *The Stane Street* (1913)

— *The Old Road* (1905)

David Caddy, *Cycling After Thomas and the English* (2013)

Zack Furness, *One Less Car: Bicycling and the politic of Automobility* (2010)

Robert Macfarlane, *The Old Ways: A Journey on Foot* (2012)

Alexis Martin, 'Physiologie de l'asphalte' in *Le Bohème* (1855)

Henry Miller, *My Bike and Other Friends* (1978)

C. E. Montague, *The Right Place* (1924)

Joe Moran, *On Roads: A Hidden History* (2009)

William Saroyan, *The Bicycle Rider in Beverly Hills* (1953)

Edward Thomas, *In Pursuit of Spring* (1914)
— *Selected Poems* (2011)
H. G. Wells, *The Wheels of Chance* (1895)

7 Coda

William Saroyan, *The Bicycle Rider in Beverly Hills* (1952)

– Acknowledgements –

I'm thankful to all at the *London Review of Books*, especially Joanna Biggs, Thomas Jones, Christian Lorentzen, Nicholas Richardson and Alice Spawls, and to Nikil Saval and *n+1*, in which some of these ideas were first aired. Bill Chidley, Ben Day, Paul Fournel, Richard Long, Robert Macfarlane and Iain Sinclair were very generous, both with their time and with their thoughts.

I am especially grateful to Damian Le Bas, Jonathan Gharraie, Edmund Gordon, Brenda Herbert, William Kraemer, Olivia Laing, Jo Lennan and Thomas Marks, who were excellent and attentive readers.

Philippa and Anne Stanners, Humphrey and Celia Bourne, Tariq and Emma Goddard, James Purdon and Kristen Treen provided shelter and company. For translations and conversations, many thanks to Charlotte Higgins, Agostino Inguscio, Alex Niven, Stephen Ross and Derry Tomlinson, and to London's couriers, who shared their stories. Thanks to Jacques Testard, who first commissioned this book, and to Kim Kremer and Karen Lockney, who finished it off. Peter Straus is a fine and attentive agent to whom I am immensely grateful. For teaching me to ride, I thank my family. Most of all I thank Natalya.

Notting Hill Editions

Notting Hill Editions is devoted to the best in essay writing. Our authors, living and dead, cover a broad range of non-fiction, but all display the virtues of brevity, soul and wit.

Our commitment to reinvigorating the essay as a literary form extends to our website, where we host the wonderful Essay Library, a home for the world's most important and enjoyable essays, including the facility to search, save your favourites and add your comments and suggestions.

To discover more, please visit
www.nottinghilleditions.com

Other titles from Notting Hill Editions*

My Katherine Mansfield Project
by Kirsty Gunn

In this lyrical essay, Gunn explores the idea of home and belonging – and the profound influence of Mansfield's work on her own creative journey.

'I began reading it and could not put it down . . . It really lives, all of it.' – John Carey

Pilgrims of the Air
by John Wilson Foster

The story of the brutal extinction of the Passenger Pigeon, once so abundant that they 'blotted out the sky'. It is also an evocative story of wild America – the ruthless exploitation of its 'commodities', and a morality tale for our times.

'Every page of this book is lit with a sense of wonder.' – Michael Longley

Nairn's Towns
by Ian Nairn, Introduced by Owen Hatherley

Sixteen short essays on Northern cities and towns in Britain. Ian Nairn (1930–1983) coined the term 'Subtopia' for the areas around cities that had been failed by urban planning.

'*Nairn's Towns* should be kept in the glove-box of every car.' – *Standpoint Magazine*

Say What You Mean: The n+1 Anthology
Edited by Christian Lorentzen

A selection from the best of *n+1*, a Brooklyn-based magazine of politics, literature and culture.

'Just when you're intellectually alone in the world, something like *n+1* falls into your hands.' – Jonathan Franzen

Questions of Travel: William Morris in Iceland
by Lavinia Greenlaw

The great Victorian William Morris was fascinated by Iceland, which inspired him to write one of the masterpieces of travel literature. The poet Lavinia Greenlaw follows in his footsteps, combining excerpts from his Icelandic writings with her own response to the country.

CLASSIC COLLECTION

The Classic Collection brings together the finest essayists of the past, introduced by contemporary writers.

Grumbling at Large – Selected Essays of J. B. Priestley
Introduced by Valerie Grove

*Beautiful and Impossible Things
– Selected Essays of Oscar Wilde*
Introduced by Gyles Brandreth

Words of Fire – Selected Essays of Ahad Ha'am
Introduced by Brian Klug

Essays on the Self – Selected Essays of Virginia Woolf
Introduced by Joanna Kavenna

*All That is Worth Remembering
– Selected Essays of William Hazlitt*
Introduced by Duncan Wu

*All NHE titles are available in the UK, and some titles are available in the rest of the world. For more information, please visit www.nottinghilleditions.com.

A selection of our titles is distributed in the US and Canada by New York Review Books. For more information on available titles, please visit www.nyrb.com.